Hoodoo

Learn About the Secret Power of Rootwork

(A Powerful Spell Book to Discover the Hidden Powers of Plants)

Paula Garcia

Published By **Matt Hall**

Paula Garcia

All Rights Reserved

Hoodoo: Learn About the Secret Power of Rootwork (A Powerful Spell Book to Discover the Hidden Powers of Plants)

ISBN 978-1-77485-625-3

No part of this guidebook shall be reproduced in any form without permission in writing from the publisher except in the case of brief quotations embodied in critical articles or reviews.

Legal & Disclaimer

The information contained in this ebook is not designed to replace or take the place of any form of medicine or professional medical advice. The information in this ebook has been provided for educational & entertainment purposes only.

The information contained in this book has been compiled from sources deemed reliable, and it is accurate to the best of the Author's knowledge; however, the Author cannot guarantee its accuracy and validity and cannot be held liable for any errors or omissions. Changes are periodically made to this book. You must consult your doctor or get professional medical advice before using any of the suggested remedies, techniques, or information in this book.

Upon using the information contained in this book, you agree to hold harmless the Author from and against any damages, costs, and expenses, including any legal fees potentially resulting from the application of any of the information provided by this guide. This disclaimer applies to any damages or injury caused by the use and application, whether directly or indirectly, of any advice or information presented, whether for breach of contract, tort, negligence, personal injury, criminal intent, or under any other cause of action.

You agree to accept all risks of using the information presented inside this book. You need to consult a professional medical practitioner in order to ensure you are both able and healthy enough to participate in this program.

Table Of Contents

Introduction 1

Chapter 1: What Hoodoo Is 5

Chapter 2: Hoodoo Spells 23

Chapter 3: How To Evoke Spirits With Hoodoo..38

Chapter 4: The Conjuring Tools Of Hoodoo..48

Chapter 5: Prayers, Psalms And Novenas As Well As The Magic Powers Of Candles..........................57

Introduction
What is Hoodoo and how can it help you?

Hoodoo refers to a folk magic that is very widespread among African Americans. You could also call it a spirituality that has been developed out of slavery. Hoodoo may be considered a type magical, but this is only one definition. They can also belong to many other types. It can be described as magic, but also an art or spiritual form.

Hoodoo could also be described to be a form African American folkmagic, with its roots mainly in European, Native American or African traditions. Evocation and evocation are two terms used to describe the practice. It is mostly found in the American Southeast. It has grown rapidly with word of mouth. Although there are many magicians who practice this magic, there isn't a scale to the art and it is open for all. Hoodoo practitioners, also known by Hoodoo physicians, used to travel to do their crafts and hired apprentices.

Many people confuse hoodoo or Magician. Magician is a West Africa-based religion. Voodoo ideas are frequently very similar to hoodoo. The practices include folk remedies as well as magic and vatication. Interpreters are typically Christians rather than Magician followers. This practice does not constitute a religion. There are many spiritual rudiments.

A lot of remedies and spells make use of objects that have been believed to possess supernatural or spiritual powers. The common components of spells include minerals, shops, animals, and bodily fluids. This is also true in other magical traditions. To make an object of a magic spell, hair, nails, or other objects can be used.

A Short History of Hoodoo

Hoodoo is a slave trade that brought many people to America from Africa Central and West Africa. Hoodoo originated in the 1800s. Hoodoo is derived form "Hudu", an ancient language and tribe from Ghana. Hoodoo could be described as a collection of practices from many

African countries like Nigeria (Kengo), Tongo, and Tongo.

Hoodoo originated as an oral tradition. This tradition was passed down or shared with family and friends. Hoodoo primarily is a solo activity.

What is the Main Difference Between Hoodoo And Voodoo

Voodoo/Voodoo/Hoodoo are distinct. Voodoo refers to spirit. Voodoo, a religion that was founded in Africa, America and the Caribbean is known as spirit. Voodoo is actually made up of two religions: Haitian Voodoo in Louisiana and Haitian Voodoo in Haiti. Louisiana Voodoo has a distinct focus on gray-gray and is very different from Haitian Voodoo.

Hoodoo may also contain the use botany, minerals, as well as parts and roots of animals. Hoodoo spells may include sleight, as well as the use a protection talisman. The doll is an image of a person made of clay, cloth or other materials. Another Hoodoo tradition is sailing. Important is the color and size for candles. They are often sprayed using oils. The candle's light will indicate the intention. It will then be lit. Hoodoo magic also can be used for divination. It is magic, which can cause chaos, crises and destruction. Hoodoo Black Magic spells could be used for chaos, disruption or destruction. Hoodoo professionals can also use white magical spells, which are either for good or disinterested.

Hoodoo, The Cultural Appropriation.

Hoodoo practices can be intrinsically linked with African American history and to the Atlantic slave exchange. This practice has been handed down to the people by their forefathers. Hoodoo magic, without African ancestry would be entirely different. Hoodoo experts, Hoodoo professionals, and Hoodoo practitioners believe that any magic performed without the ancestral connection should not count as Hoodoo.

Wiccans have a tendency to use influences from other cultures, places and times in their magical practices.

Chapter 1: What Hoodoo Is

Hoodoo can be described as traditional magic, and it is very common among African Americans. Hoodoo was first created by various Africans who were imprisoned. These Africans were engaged with spiritual practices, which they brought with them to the enslaved countries.

Hoodoo could also be called rootwork, conjure or rootwork. Hoodoo practitioners can use many tools, including herbs, roots, candles and roots. Hoodoo doesn't have to be about harming people. It can be used to protect and heal.

Hoodoo will use certain items that are considered personal concerns. Personal concerns are items that are specific to you such as hair, bones, blood or nail clippings. They can be mixed together with ingredients to produce a positive or negative result. The items can be placed in the conjure pots or bags with herbs, roots and graveyard dirt. Sometimes they're ground till they turn into powder. To create misfortune, they are buried below the person's shoes. To prevent a curse being enacted, you can lighten your combed, uncombed, or fallen hair. This will ensure that the conjurer does not make a powder to expel the curse.

A brief history and description of Hoodoo

Hoodoo, a group of spiritual practices and beliefs that were created in the different countries by enslaved Africans, is known as the "hoodoo" system. Hoodoo is a popular North American practice. Hoodoo was practiced, used tools, and everything that went with it were kept secret by slave masters. From the early 16th to the 19th centuries, more than 12 million slaved Africans belonging to different ethnic groups were shipped to America as part of the transatlantic Slave Trade mission. Between 1619 & 1808, the United States witnessed the slave trade. About 500,000 African slaves were then sent to America between 1619-1808.

During slavery trade, the American slave traders brought Igbos, Yorubas to the United States. Hoodoo was invented by the enslaved once they had been brought to the United States.

Hoodoo was created for them to survive the harsh conditions that they were subject to. It was a means to resist and survive against slavery.

The African American community did no have any psychological or medical aids to help the slaves. They had to rely on each other for survival. Hoodoo was a protection system for the enslaved Africans. Different African ethnicities were employed in the same plantations. Hoodoo was created when the various African ethnicities merged to form a larger group called African Americans. These religions unites slaves. Each brought his or her own version of rootwork that was later used to create Hoodoo. It was used also to conjure liberty.

Hoodoo: Practices

Hoodoo initiations

After they have found the spirits, they initiate the process. They combine Hoodoo worship with practices from Christendom. After they have been initiated they will be accepted into hoodoo worshippers.

Spirit mediation

Hoodoo may also allow others to access certain forces to make a difference in their lives. Hoodoo was created in order to help people succeed in different areas. This includes love, money, work, health, and many other areas.

You can use different parts, animals, herbs, and a possession of the person you wish to gain favor from. This includes candles, incenses, colored candles, and hair. Some spiritual tools may bring protection, healing or luck. Hoodoo, for example, can conjure up the situation if you don't want to see your husband or wife separated. For example, you could get a rabbit's forefoot, nine strands or hairs removed from the head, a loadingstone, and put them in a red flannel bag before burying them under the front door.

Offering

Hoodoo offers another form of practice: offering. This practice consisted of leaving food behind for family members who had died. It is used to feed the spirits and conjure up other spirits. This offering honors ancestors or the spirit of death.

Difference between Hoodoo (Voodoo)

Hoodoo is a term that reminds one of African black magicianry. Voodoo is another. Although they may be used interchangeably, these terms do not refer to the same thing. They have very little in common, though they share the same roots.

Voodoo derives its name from the French word, "vodu". It is an ancient pagan religion containing a mix tradition and beliefs. Voodoo originated in Haiti and is still being practiced by many Haitians. According to this religion, believers believe in God as a creator. He is thought to be a spirit that does no interference in the daily lives of human beings. Bondye is the name God. Voodooists aim to please the spirit Loa. There are plenty of options for every section of life. To please the spirits and make life easier, they participate in many practices like dancing and music. BoKor refers to Voodoo priests who perform rituals that intercede for the loas. Europeans who practiced this religion were taught it by French slaves during the eighteenth century. They then tried to pass it along to the rest of the world.

Hoodoo is magic which combines traditions from both African and American cultures. Hoodoo in English is generally described as a spell chanted upon someone. Hoodoo uses a more magical ritual which has been passed down through the generations. Hoodoo practitioners do away with the practice of voodoo.

Below are the key differences between Hoodoo/Voodoo.

Hoodoo is magic. Voodoo focuses on religion.

They have Bondye (Voodoo) as their creator. Hoodoo doesn't have any such creator.

Voodoo, a religion some Haitians practice, is known as the "Voodoo Religion". The Europeans introduced religion to the country. Hoodoo, however, was practiced in different

African American slaves. They brought their gods with them.

Voodoo (pronounced "voodoo") is a well-known religion. It's used to predict and simplify life. They just try to please a spirit named loas.

Hoodoo practitioners are known as root physicians. They have been called to rule their enemies, bring ill fortune to their enemies, or to bring good luck to themselves.

Redbrick dust

Redbrick, which is used for magic and spell casting, is one of the most infamous hoodoo tricks. Red brick dust can be used to protect your home spiritually. It brings you lots of good luck, prosperity, and more. Red brick dust's name might give you some idea of its meaning. The red bricks provide the source of the red brick dust. Redbrick is also called reddening. It has been used for many years as a modernized version of the sacred redochre that was used during ancient rituals.

Red Brick Dust can be very powerful. It protects the home. There are some properties within it that make it very powerful for conjuring protection magic.

Bricks have been used in the construction of homes for over a century. The main purpose of bricks is to protect it from the environment. Bricks that have been fired last longer and are stronger building materials.

Bricks are made with earth materials such clay, clay, and limestone. The earth element is very important to protect the home. Redbrick is also rich in iron, which is an extremely powerful metal.

Since antiquity, the color red has been closely associated with the worlds of the ancestors/dead. The ancestors represent one of the most important protectors. Although brick does have protective qualities, physical qualities found in the earth also act as protection.

Let me show how you can make red brick dust and conjure magical protection in your house.

Make red brick dust with the following supplies

Red Brick

Flaccid hard surface

Hammer of metallic metal

A small amount if whiskey or rum.

Funnel

Mortar, pestle

Jar or vessel

Mask and goggles (so dust doesn't get into your eyes)

Guidelines

Lay a piece thick of paper or cardboard over the hard, flat surface that you have in your backyard. The surface will be hammered against, so the cardboard or paper should not be placed on glass or tables. The cardboard will contain the broken bricks even after they are broken into pieces.

You can place the brick in its middle and then sprinkle whiskey or rum onto it. Don't put too much rum on it. Sprinkle it lightly. The rum should be an offering to the brick to do the work that you have asked it to.

Make sure to pray for protection.

You can cover your face with a mask or handkerchief, and your eyes with goggles. It will protect your eye and face from the dust, red bricks, or other debris that could be hitting you.

Start to break down the brick with your hammer. Use the pieces that you have to determine how much pressure to apply.

Keep praying over your brick while you use the hammer to cut it into small pieces.

Once you have broken the bricks up into small pieces put the bricks in the mortar.

Use your pestle to start pounding the bricks. Once the bricks are ground to a powder, you can grind them. Then, grind the remaining bricks to make a powder.

Continue praying for protection of your brick. To transfer brick dusk into a container, use your funnel.

You can label the jar to keep it handy until you need it.

How to use your red brick dust in a jar/vessel

Red brick dust can also be used to cleanse the door.

Apply the protective herb powder to the thresholds.

Prepare a reddening blend of ammonia and urine. Wash the doors, thresholds, and windows with it. This is a great way of conjuring prosperity and protection.

If you're looking to make more, mix the red brick with cinnamon sugar and brown sugar. You can then use this mixture to wash your front doors.

It is possible to get an old brick and make red brick dust. There are many places where you can find them. If you are lucky enough to live in an old home, they might be found in your backyard. You can also search eBay for it or on a dumpsite.

MOJO bag

Mojo is an African American belief system in Hoodoo. It is an amulet with two or more magical items that is stored in a flannel case. It is known as prayer within a bag. The majority of conjure bag materials are red flannel. But, the contents or charms inside each bag will vary depending on the person conjuring them. A mojo to draw your love will have different ingredients for luck and protection. Gravyard dirt can be combined with herbs, roots and coins. It also includes animal parts, minerals and amulets. Some mojo bags were used to create bad luck for slave masters as well as protect them from danger.

There is a way you can create a powerful and good mojo. You must prepare a ritual for making the mojo preparation successful. The mojo must have life and be capable of working for its design. Smoking incense and candles are two options. Or you could simply breathe on the mojo to bring it into being. It is possible to chant prayers. After you have completed the ritual, the mojo should be fed or clothed with a liquid such as perfume, alcohol, or bodily fluids.

To ensure that the mojo is still working, you need to do it.

Black cat bone

Hoodoo magic uses the black cats bone as a luck charm. This luck charm is also used in Hoodoo magic. It causes positive things to happen in an individual's daily life including invisibility and protection, good luck, magic, rebirth, and even rebirth. A mojobag can be used to carry a well-prepared and prepared bone for the work that it is intended to do. The bone should be kept in the mouth.

There are many methods to make a black catbone

Once you have caught a cat in black, you cook it alive in water at midnight. This will allow the practitioner to care for the bones and facilitate the cooking process. A bone can be modified to perform any task desired, and it is sufficient to hold all the magic powers. A few rituals were required to determine which bone is best to use.

Fasting can be used to obtain a black catbone. Fasting before you catch your cat is possible. Once you have boiled your cat, take it out from the pot. Then taste the bone. The user (hoodooists), then tastes the bone. He will then decide which one tastes the best as the best for him.

Mirror is another way to determine the magical bones. The practitioner will determine the right one by placing the bone into the mirror.

A river can be another way to find the right bones. The correct bone is the one floating on the top of the river.

Four thieves vinegar

Another popular Hoodoo magic ingredient is Four Thieves Vinegar. While this is a potion magic, the four-thineves potion can also be associated to plague outbreaks throughout Europe in the 16th-17th centuries. To prevent illness, you can use four Thieves vinegar.

Uses of the four Thieves vinegar

It can also be used to treat diseases and sickness.

It is a protection magick.

The potion works by banishing those whom we don't wish to see again.

You can use this to remove negative energy from your home or life.

How to make four Thieves vinegar potion

Four Thieves' vinegar recipe is unique in that you cannot use the same ingredients for different purposes. The type of spell that you wish to cast determines which recipe you will use. Sage or lavender can be used to make protection spells. If you're looking for banishing spells then red and/or black pepper ingredients are best. There are many herbs you can add to your recipe, including clove, camphor. rue, rosemary and others. A health expert suggests that the mix can be drunk in small doses.

Ingredients needed to make four bottles of Thieves' vinegar

A mason jar

One teaspoon of Lavender

One teaspoon of dried thyme

One teaspoon of Sage

Mince 1 teaspoon garlic

One cup apple cider vinegar

Combine all the ingredients in a large jar. Stir them together. Keep the mixture out on the windowsill until the sun and moon shine down and bless it. After one day, you can take the container out. The solids can be strained. Put it into a jar.

Gofer powder

Hoodoo was practiced by African American Hoodooists using gofer powder. It is a powder which can be used to cast a spell. It is usually used in concoctions that are made of natural ingredients. These can be used to cause trouble, harm or kill the enemy. Hoodoists mostly use gofer to cause blindness or swelling in an enemy.

You can make gofer powder using many different ingredients. Some people use graveyard soil and snakeskin. Others might use ash. It can be either yellowish-grey or black dust after it has been ground. It all depends upon the ingredients. Sometimes goofer powder can be used to cast love spells. Goofer powder will incite spirits to make the target fall madly in love with you. A protective spell can be made by mixing graveyard dirt left over from a loved one with pepper and salt.

Foot Track Magic

Foot track magic is the practice of spraying powders along the target's path. You'll throw powder on the target and they'll suffer all sorts of problems and abnormalities. The powder's toxic components will get absorbed via the feet. Once the poison gets to the target, it can cause back problems, water retention and difficulties walking, especially in the legs. Only a rootworker could remove the foot track magic.

There are two possible ways to perform foot track magic. One is direct, the other is sympathetic. The direct method occurs when the substance that was thrown onto the ground is buried and the target touches it.

The second way is to capture the target's footprint. Either by collecting dust from the target's real footprint, or taking the shoe or sock you have and adding powder to it.

Chapter 2: Hoodoo Spells

Hoodoo chants no longer work. The spell is performed using selections of the Bible. Psalms or other scriptures can be read from the Bible. Psalm 91, for instance, can be used to eliminate jinx. After reading aloud the Psalm three time, keep your eyes on your candle and your mind focused on it. The application process of spells are very straightforward. You don't have to go through any stress before you can use the spells to bind the target. This is your hoodoo content. Use your instinct to discover a few methods and apply them.

Banishing spells

Banishing spells can be used to rid yourself of an enemy, or get rid your neighbor. They can be used to banish emotions or illness, lover jealousy, strange spirit, and others. The moon's waning is the best time for this activity.

You can banish sickness spell

Salt in large amounts is necessary to banish illness. You can carry the salt around and throw it in a fire. The flames instantly will turn to blue.

To see the illness go away, fix your eyes on the flames in the blue. As soon as you visualize the illness being eliminated from your body, start to repeat these words.

"Sickness does not burn, but good-health returns."

You can also use the illness spell for other people.

Let the enemy go spell

You can either buy a multipurpose hoodoo toy doll or make it yourself. The doll should reflect your intent.

Finally, you will write down a statement on a piece a paper that states "I am here in order to remove negative influences" Right now (mention you name) is exerting a very negative influence on me. I ask Manman Brit and Baron Samedi for their assistance.

Place the statement into the doll

Pick up the doll, take it to a distant place, dig a well, and place the doll inside. Finally, cover the doll with earth and burn it.

As the fire is blazing, say, "ashes in ashes, dust in dust, enemy far away,"

You can find dirt by looking around, and then you can use that dirt to cover the doll. It's best to leave the place and never look back.

Bend over spells

Bend over spells will make someone bend under your command. The person will do what you ask. These spells can help you get your boss, friend and family to treat you well and respect you. You can use them to dominate someone sexually. To make someone else do what is best for you, use the spells listed below.

Choose the largest stick candles you can find. Place some oil in your palm. Then, twist the candle using both your hands.

You can then roll your candle into a powder of salt-camphor. Keep the candle lit and left to burn until the end. After it's been lit for the third time, remove the powdered mixture from the candle and place it in a spot where the person you wish it to be cast upon will pass.

Binding spells

Binding spells are used to prevent someone from harming or you. You can create charms to bind your enemy.

Charm to bind an enemy

You should look for cobwebs within your home and collect them together. Next, apply them to a piece or black cloth in an messy manner.

Then, look for the deadly flu. Find a sheet of paper, and then write the following word.

"North, South, East, West.

Spider's Web is his best way to find him

East, West, North, South.

He should hold his arms straight and not let go of his mouth.

His eyes should be closed and his mouth must be clenched.

Secure him with the ropes to death.

Your paper should be folded four times. Then wrap the packet with the fly and webs inside the small black cloth. Wrap it tightly with a long string, leaving enough cord to hang from a desk.

If it is not covered in dust, please leave it at home. After that, you will need to find a place to put it.

Binding spell

You should look for a guardian-angel candle and then find peace oil to use as a dressing.

Light the candle and enjoy a few drops from frankincense essential oil.

Start by getting a pen.

Then, look for thread and place it in a pit in the ground under a faraway tree.

Then, read Psalms 133, 139 nine-times each.

Healing spells

This spell will help you to heal physical pain.

You will need amethyst pieces or fluorite along with visualization skills.

Seek out a tranquil and quiet spot, then go there to get rid of your negative thoughts. Grab the fluorite/amethyst in your hands and place it next to the one that is bothering you.

You can also hold it in your right-hand if you feel the pain in the middle. Bring the soothing light to your feet. Next, bring it up slowly to your head. Then silently repeat the words.

"Bright Light, Shining Light"

"Heal my pains with all thy might."

Continue saying the words until the light moves up through your body. You can then stretch your neck out and fill your head with light. Now, return to the place where you feel the pain. Channel all of your healing energy to this area.

You can do this over and over until you master it. You will feel better as time goes by. You can end the spell by repeating the verse, and at the last saying "so it is."

Love spells

Many experts advise against casting love spells on a single person. These spells can be used to attract the love of all people. The universe will then bring you the right person, and not try to manipulate it.

The attraction to love charm

If the moon is full, look for a sterling ring and wrap it with a clean white fabric. Find a small, undiscovered hole and place the ring there.

Once you've done that, you can visualize the kind lover you want.

"Blessed mother fair and true

This is the Gift I Offer to You

Get it to shine!

Bring a lover.

Next, say the words "let it come true" at the end.

It is best to keep the ring hidden until the full Moon. Now, you can find the ring and put it in your hand. The lover will be attracted towards you.

Attractive love spell

This spell is used to attract the person that you want to begin a relationship. The spell is especially effective when used during the full Moon or when the moon is waxing. To make the spell effective, you'll need the following.

Pink candle

Toothpick

A favorite scent or essential oil.

With a toothpick, shape the heart from the candle.

Place the candle on your windowsill. Let the moonlight dance in the heart. Place the essential oil/perfume on top of the candle.

Leave the candle alone to burn. Keep the perfume close at hand and spray it everywhere you go. For the spell to work even better, repeat the words each time you spray your fragrance on your body.

Ex-spell back

The spell can bring back your ex-love. This is what you need for the spell.

You can buy pieces of paper

Your lover accidentally left a dirty sock or any of his belongings.

Fresh basil

Glass of water

Fresh basil

A glass of water

You can write three times the name of your lover on a piece paper.

You will need to look for soft ground. Dig a small hole in it. Add a note with your name to the hole and then add a sock or other personal item.

Light up a red candle. Leave it burning. You can also add a small amount of sweet basil to a glass. Light the candle at noon. Leave it burning until one o clock.

Pin your candle flames. Light the candle and allow it to burn for seven hours.

After the candle has been lighted, place the barrel over the hole. After you place it, shake it three more times to activate the spirit.

"Tumba Walla, Bumba Walla, bring (name your lover) home to me."

Money spells

Take all the buckeyes and wrap around a Dollar bill.

Make sure you have fast luck oil on hand and apply it to your skin. Keep them in your pocket, so they can draw money.

Hoodoo Rituals

Hoodoo ritual, also known as spiritual bathing, can be used to cleanse both your physical and spiritual bodies. Ritual bathing helps to battle fatigue, negativity fear, depression and anxiety. Ritual bathing is meant to revive spirits after bad experiences. Ritual bathing must be done according to the purpose.

The following is a general guideline to ritual bathing.

Before you take a hot bath, you should bless the water, and invoke the healing spirits in a way that is meaningful for you.

Get into the tube and make sure you mention your problem as you go.

The ritual bath should take at most 15 minutes. You can sit, sing, or meditate and visualize the solution. Do whatever it takes to comfort you.

Imagine the water going down the drain and your problem being washed away by the water. Just as you're about the end of pouring the last drop, pronounce the word "let It Be So."

When you get out of your bathtub, be sure to rinse it with saltwater. Regular salt works well, but sea salt is better. Salt water is best for cleaning any objects that you have in your tub.

To make the ritual bath enjoyable and comforting, light some of your favorite incense.

Before you take a routine bath, it is a good idea to have a regular one. To achieve maximum effects, you should not remain in a bath ritual for more that thirty minutes.

Negativity can be prevented by taking magical baths

To eliminate negative energies and unwanted thoughts, you can use the ritual baths.

One tablespoon of ammonia can also be added to your bathwater. The bath should be used only once every three month.

If you wish to wash your clothes daily or weekly, you could also use a tablespoonful of ammonia. It will take out any negative energy.

Add Florida water fragrance to your bathwater.

Add hyssop

Rue

Rosemary

Rock salt

A small amount of Florida water-based Cologne

Holy water

Money-drawing Ritual

This is a safer method to draw money. It's also an excellent way for energy balance to be added to and taken away.

Ingredients

Permanent marker

Dollar bills

Steps

Grab a dollar bill and draw the blessings that you want on it with a permanent pen. Write, "May I live a rich life."

Locate a gluestick and find somewhere to drop it. It will appear as an accident. It's an intentional spell. However, reap and sow will still be active.

Hoodoo recipes

Attraction Love Oil

Hoodoo attraction is used to draw love. You can mix the parts of the following items together.

Rose Geranium Essential Oil

Rose Otto Essential Oil of Roses

Vanilla oil

Sandalwood oil

Rose Fragrance, Synthetic

Lavender oil

Overlook oil

Other people can make a wish with the potent oil. The oil is able to be bent over to disarm any bossy person and return the evil spirit to its sender.

The following recipe will help you make your bend over oil

Licorice root

Calamus Root

Essential oil for bergamot

Blend a few frankincense grains in almond oil and add a little vitamin E.

Come to me oil

Roses

Jasmine

Lemon oil

The rose petals are a great way to show your love. Patchouli will increase the passion.

Chapter 3: How To Evoke Spirits With Hoodoo

Hoodoo practitioners perform the act of seeking salvation to ask for their souls' salvation so that the church can accept them. The spiritual leader will guide the process. Once the follower has done some rituals, he will make the announcement to the members. The announcement will be followed by singing and cheers. Shout can be translated as dancing or movement in the Kaaba.

Members will dance in an anticlockwise motion to invoke the spirits and ancestors. African Americans dance for the spirit. It is possible to be possessed or touched in this way by the Holy God. African Americans combine Hoodoo and Christian religion in a unique way. Some of the hoodoo traditions are used in churches.

As they are performing the ring call, African Americans will place their feet on a flat surface to create static electricity. Connecting with the spiritual energies, they invoke the creator's spirit since He created it, and bring down his spirit. This practice involves singing or clapping. As the spiritual energies rise, someone will be pulled into the middle by the spirit invoked. The spirit will now enter the body to direct the gathering.

How to use the law to attract your desires

The law is universal and works throughout the universe. It is a universal rule that applies to all aspects in your life, money included, as well as relationships. The law is all about who you attract. You can also control and see the result of your energy and focus. This law does not require that you be spiritually advanced to use it. Instead, it benefits your mental health and helps you connect with your dreams.

This law is applicable to everyone. You can learn a lot from the law. To see the changes you desire in your life, you have to change what you believe and your reality. The law behind the law of attraction is simple: you can move forward and create the reality you want, provided you're free from all obstacles.

Apply the law to attract principles to your relationships if you want to find love. These steps can help you create a lasting and good relationship. There are many possible reasons that you don't feel the love and connection you desire. You must be truthful with yourself. Imagine how you feel about someone. The five laws that attract you to create a life you love and a relationship that is fulfilling are the best ways to start manifesting your dreams.

Hoodoo is a law of attraction.

Glass with candle

Roses petals

Follow these steps to achieve the law o' attraction.

Set your intentions clear

You should make it clear that this is a commitment to a relationship. Clarify your intention if it is unclear. It is easy to do this by writing down your statement. Find the phrase that is most in line with your intention. A simple way to make your intention lighter is to say something like, "I am ready and willing for love to come into my life. And I open my hearts to meet a lover." It is possible to repeat the statement repeatedly in order to ingrain it in your subconscious.

Visualize your dream partner

Your dream partner is the one you choose to live with. Write down what you value and what are the most important characteristics of your partner. You must write down the things you desire in a relationship and the words you use to describe it. A clear guideline will help you create an image of your future partner. Use words that both of you can visualize. Be open to the love mystery, but keep this in mind.

Your partner should have the same qualities as you.

They say like attracts like. The energy around you is the key to all of the universe's energy. You can think about the essential characteristics that make a person a great person. Then, think about how you will foster these traits in your own personal life. If humility is important, you should be more accepting of yourself. If you are passionate about humor, then go on the adventure! This will help you find your ideal partner. When you open your heart to meet someone who shares your interests and has the same priorities, life will grow in your heart and you will be more attentive to that special person.

Show your love

Your love will attract the love of your life. Love who you truly are. When you love yourself, negative thoughts are replaced by positive ones. If you love yourself every single day, you will make more connections in your life. Being able to love yourself will prepare you to be in a happy and healthy space to meet your lover.

How to use attraction law towards your career goals (Job).

Ever wondered why certain people seem to be so successful? One thing they did know was the law od attraction. The energy in our thoughts is what can make a difference in our lives. It will attract whatever you give your attention, energy, focus, and energy into your life.

Be clear about your goals

You must first think about the job you want to achieve your dream career. It's hard to reach your goal without one. Ask questions. Why would you like to make a change in career? What is the one thing you don't like about your previous job? Let go of your ego and look for opportunities to make positive changes. The future you envision is five to ten years away. Start a new career by joining a Board or starting a hustle. Once you have identified your goal, take a note of it and share it.

Focus on your future

If you're looking for your dream job, it is possible to shift your focus from what you don't want to do to what you do. It's easy to get consumed with negative thoughts about your job. Focusing on what you don't want will lead to more of these situations in your life. You can focus on your true goal, and replace the bad image with the good.

Believe in your intention

It doesn't matter how often you repeat affirmations to your self in the morning or at night, if you don't believe in them, you won't reach that goal. Believing is a choice. Although believing in your big dream can be difficult, it is vital. Each day, practice visualization.

Take the appropriate action

Dreams without action are just that: dreams. To get your dream job, you need to keep your skills current. You can apply for certification classes.

How to use attraction law to make your money work

Truth is, anyone would desire to build wealth and live a happy, fulfilled life. Many people do not know how manage money. They have a difficult time achieving their wealth and financial goals. To change your beliefs about wealth, you can use the law of attraction.

Follow the below steps to manifest your money.

Be aware of your beliefs about money

This law is only possible if you take note of your money beliefs and make changes to them. All people are born with the belief of limiting their money thinking from childhood. You have probably heard of this belief before. This belief would have been commonplace.

To use this law of attraction you must address your negative views about money. You will easily create the habits and thought patterns necessary to make money.

Visualize a boost in your wealth like you already have it

The law o' attraction states that things that you believe in and project into the world will attract to your life. To attract money, visualize it. Visualizing means to imagine yourself in a place with plenty of money. Visualize the money you are about to receive as if it is already yours. This will lead to a mindset that is focused on abundance. Have you ever wondered why wealthy people have more wealth?

They consider the money they don't own as their own. They see the lack of money as abundance and not scarcity.

The Hoodoo Altar

You must have a space to perform rituals before you start any good practice. It should be quiet and free from distractions. Place a flat, smooth surface, such as a table or box, on the ground. You can either set aside a part of the floor for your altar, or use the drawer from a dresser to store all of your ritual supplies. You'll need some items to personalize and some things to put on your altar.

To cover the altar's surface, get some cloth.

Place two white candles backwards on the altar at both ends.

All images and figures of saints may be placed at the back side of the two white candle.

Place your incense-burner in the middle and front of your altar.

Keep a bowl with water that you have blessed in the area right above your incense maker. Fresh cut flowers, a piece or stones can be included, along with a dish of graveyard dirt and salt.

Don't put anything you don't want on your altar. Altars can be anything from very simple to extremely elaborate. Make sure to clean all containers and bowls with saltwater.

Chapter 4: The Conjuring Tools Of Hoodoo

It is necessary to conjure, or do rootwork. Without these tools, it is impossible to create a spell and a potion. They are just like the potion. Here's a list of the supplies and tools needed to conjure Hoodoo.

Bottles/jars: You could recycle jars/bottles of all sorts - pickles/perfumes, baby foods.

Baskets are useful for transporting the items.

Cauldron: A large pot of iron for turning potions

Charcoal blocks can be used to light incense. Pure bamboo charcoals made in Japan are also available.

Droppers: These are drops for essential oils.

Chinaware: It is a mini-fireplace made of Chinaware. They come in many sizes so they can be lit or used for ritual incense.

The kettle can be used to heat water.

Measurement stainless steel and spoons

Funnel is used to transfer oil, liquids, and particles.

Plastic bags for storage

Mortar-and-pill to grind resins.

Scissors for cutting cord, string and twine

Pruning shears can be used to harvest plants and herbs

Straining devices, such as a cheesecloth oder stainless steel sieve.

Hemp cord or hemp twine to tie mojo bag and herb knots

Herb storage containers include brown paper bags and dark glass containers.

The incense

It is important that you have the right incenses for your particular tools. Below is a list containing incenses or resins used in Hoodoo.

Hoodoo contains myrrh (and frankincense) which are vital in African healing.

Camphor: It is purifying and dreams incense.

Aloeswood and spiritual incense can be used for love spells. These can invoke the assistance of evil spirit, but keep them away from your reach.

Copal can be used as a fumigant. This holy incense, known as copal resin, comes out in sticks or cones. It can be used as a blessing for oneself, others, to cast love spells or to heal respiratory disease.

Dragon'sblood: A powdered resin that can be used in luck to prevent evil. It can bring luck in love or money.

Jasmine - Spiritual incense can be made from dried flowers tops.

Frankincense (or spiritual incense): It is a resin-like fumigant which comes out as a stick or cone of resin. It can be used to invoke spirits and increase concentration, protection, blessings, and protection.

Lavender - The lavender is used for attracting the same sex. It can be made from loose flowers, sticks or cones and is spiritual incense.

Myrrh: Holy incense, made from resins or sticks and cones. It can be used to promote relaxation, peace, healing, and good health. Myrrh may be used to encourage sensual love. It can also be used to anoint, bless, protect, and honor the moon as well as the creator goddess.

Pink Rose is associated with Erzulie Freda

Patchouli is a fumigant, similar to spiritual incense. It can also be used to invoke protection and blessings.

Rose Otto - It can be used to create live works, but it is very costly. It is associated to Oshun and Aphrodite.

Sandalwood can be purchased as powder or in chips in sticks, cones, and in small pieces. It is an aphrodisiac that can be used for protection and peace.

Ritual use

Incense can be used ritually to purify. It is effective in getting rid of negative energy. It can increase energy and get rid of any emotional baggage. Incense can also help to instill a sense of spirit. Incense can be offered to bring down the spirits. Incense can be used if you are trying to end a relationship or to remove someone from your life.

A little bit of the purification candle can be burned in every corner of your property. In the shower, you can feel the water purifying your skin. To prevent any negative energy entering your house, you can place a line of clear tape in front. Mix incense and water, then use it to wash the house. You can also mix incense with kosher sea salt and place it in the middle your house. Your home will feel purified and clean if you refresh it every seven days. You can also combine them in a bath, place one in each stocking, then throw it in the tube. As you are reciting Psalms 23-91, burn a little of the incense.

Hoodoo dolls

How to make an adorable doll

First, trace a template onto a piece. Next, cut it. The template does not need to be perfect. However, it should look similar to a Hoodoo doll.

Cut the material that you intend to use. As a guide, use the template to cut the felt. Finally, remove the pins. Because of the way you want to make the hoodoo dolls, do not add extra seams.

The button can be found in the left eye of the felt material. A needle with black embroidery floss can be used to create a white button on your right-hand side. Continue sewing, but don't cut off the floss.

Stick an X in the left ear. Check that the thread is adequate and do not use different embroidery floss. The first eye may be slightly smaller than the second. Add your final X to the back.

Draw a straightline for the base of the mouth. Move the mouth forward from one eye to the next and sew at each end. To ensure that your needle doesn't fall below the left eye, bring it up using the back side of your felt. The thread should be kept close together, so it doesn't get squeezed.

You can make your mouth look like it has been closed by using four to five vertical line. The Hoodoo's mouth opens to the left. The line should pass through the horizontal lines. Begin and end at the horizontal line. Add some space for evenness. The floss can be knotted or cut.

Now join the pieces, letting the wrong side face in. The embroidery floss can be used to sew the pieces together. You will need to push the needle up the left side. Then wrap the needle around the back of the doll. Pull the needle up via the felt. It should be just a little above the first stitch. For the purpose of stuffing the doll with polyester, leave some space.

After sewing it, stuff it with any extra space.

Next, finish sewing the doll by closing it.

Baptize the doll

It is necessary to baptize the doll in order to activate its powerful magical ability. Consecrate it. Consecration means to open up and tap into the divine force in order to access solutions and possible wishes, miracles, and other possibilities. Your doll can be made sacred by being connected to the divine force through the ritual. Consecration removes all negative energy that might be attached to an object. It eliminated all energy that was associated with anyone who touched the doll/material.

Materials required for ritual

Hoodoo doll

White candles

Some cedar

Sage

To burn the incense, you will need an incense transporter.

Place the doll on top of the altar. Sprinkle salt all over the doll and say the following:

"I consecrate You to the element Earth."

Pass the doll over the incense.

"I consecrate You to the Air."

Pass the doll to the candle flame.

"I consecrate You to the Fire."

Sprinkle the doll with water, and say:

"I consecrate You to the Water."

Place the object on your altar. Imagine the Divine shining through your hands on your doll.

"I thusforth call this doll _____" and declare it to be charged with the power of spirit, air water, fire, and Earth. You can only use it for good. This is my will and divine law. May it serve your well in this world as well as in all other worlds. Let it so be!

Chapter 5: Prayers, Psalms And Novenas As Well As The Magic Powers Of Candles

Prayer

Hoodoo's religion is all about prayer. Some practitioners only use the Apostle's Creed. Other practitioners use everything. It doesn't matter if it is spoken in an orderly manner; it all depends on society. You'll find some prayer for specific purposes and some critical prayers.

You can start by reading the Apostle's Creed. Then, go on to say "Hail Mary", ask God to bless you home, and finally, pray the Lord's prayers. An example of a prayer is to the African powers.

Below are examples for the prayers.

The Apostle's Creed

I believe God, the Father Almighty.

The creator of heavens & earth.

and in Jesus Christ His only Son, our Lord:

Who was the Holy Ghost conceived?

Mary, the Virgin Mary was born

Pontius Pisate's sufferings

He was crucified, buried and died.

He fell into hell.

He rose from the dead on the third day.

He ascended into Heaven

He sits at God Almighty's right hand.

He will judge the living and death from thereon.

I believe in Holy Spirit, the holy Catholic Church.

The communion between saints

Forgiveness for sins

The resurrection of our bodies

You will live a happy, fulfilled life.

Amen.

Hail Mary

Hail Mary, full and complete with grace

The Lord is beside you

Blessed art you among women

Jesus says, "Blessed is the fruit that thy breasts produce."

Holy Mary Mother of God, pray that we sinners be saved

Now and in our hour of death, Amen.

Home Blessing

Bless my home

Let love flourish here

Let wisdom grow,

Peace, peace, and happiness are yours!

Bless my home

Let it preserve my life

Let it nourish me.

Enjoy peace and tranquility!

Blessed is my home

The Lord's Prayer

Our Father, who art in heaven

Hallowed be Thy name.

Your kingdom has come, you will rule!

on earth as it does in heaven.

This day is your daily bread.

And forgive us all our trespasses

We will forgive anyone who trespasses against us

We must not be led into temptation

Please deliver us from evil

For thine are power, the kingdom, glory

Forever. Amen.

Prayer for the Home

We beseech O Lord.

Visit this home

It is important to get out of all the traps laid by the enemy.

Let Your holy angels live there

Keep us safe;

Let Your blessing be with us always

Through Christ our Savior. Amen.

Prayer to the Seven African Powers

Oh, Seven African Powers. You are so very close to the Divine Savior.

humility, I kneel down before you to ask your intercession in the Great

Spirit. Please accept my petition and grant me your peace and prosperity. Please remove all obstacles and obstacles that hinder my progress. I trust in the words, "ask to receive" Amen. Please sign the petition.

Prayer to St. Joseph For Protection

Gracious St. Joseph. Protect me and your family

You saved the Holy to save your family from evil.

Family. Keep me forever united,

Christ Love, ever serious in

imitation of the virtue of the Blessed

Lady, your faithful and loving spouse.

Loving you with all your heart. Amen.

So that he can protect your family, you could place a St. Joseph-style statue in your kitchen

Everyday.

Novenas

The Novena (a prayer) can be used in conjunction with seven-day candles. These candles are made of glass and can burn for seven straight days. Before lighting the candle you should pray for your intentions and the saint. The prayers will be printed on your glass container. The novena must be said every day at the same hour. If you decide to say the prayers after 7 pm each day, continue that pattern for maximum results.

When praying the Novena start by making the sign on the cross. After that, you can say "In the Names of the Father, the Son, or the Holy Spirit". You should say "Amen" before starting the novena praying. Make sure your petition is unique so you are able to keep any vows.

St. Expedito – Oh. Glorious Martyr. Protector. St. Expedito! We offer our humble assistance.

To have luck and prosperity in our lives, to ensure that the sick get well

The guilty get pardoned and the just be kept, while those who abandon this valley go to jail

There is a place for tears in the Light of the Lord, and the souls the dearly departed are at rest

in peace. (Mention the request). Amen.

St. Jude - Most Holy Apostle, St. Jude. Faithful Servant Of Jesus.

Prayers for me in times of such despair and great need. Bring immediate help. I will continue to consider you my most special and most powerful patron. (Make a sign of the cross.

Miraculous Mother, Oh, Miraculous Mutter! With inspired confidence I

Invoke thee for your loving-kindness and mercy so that my needs and troubles can be met with thy eternal help.

Do you agree to my wish? Amen.

St. Michael – Oh glorious Archangel St. Michael. Watch over me my whole life. Protect me against the demons. Assist me especially at the hour I die. Receive a favorable verdict and assist me with all of my needs. Amen.

St. Barbara. Oh St. Barbara. Your last words to Christ Jesus.

Everyone who invoked this spell had their heads cut off by a sword.

Your sins may be forgotten when they are redeemed by His Holy Name. Please support me in my trials, comfort me and intercede on my behalf for my family. Thank you for your prayers.

The Psalms

Hoodoo makes use of Bible Psalms, which can be used to conjure spells or conjure them. The Psalms spoken by King David contained hidden words that can create magical effects when they are spoken aloud.

The book of Psalms contains 150 Psalms. Each Psalm includes a song of religious significance. Psalms used in hoodoo magical is similar to conjuring the Solomonic heritage. The subject matter and effect of your passage affects how the scripture works. You might have to change psalm 60 if you want fortune in your home.

Thou hast been my refuge and my strong tower against the enemies. I will always be in Thy Tabernacle; I trust in Thy wings.

If you're travelling at night and need protection, you can invoke psalm 122.1;

I will be able to see the hills with my eyes, where my help comes.

Psalm 64 helps you avoid accidents. Psalm28 is for exorcising demons.

Psalm 101 is a good place to start if you are looking for love. Psalms 119 and 119 are good for getting money.

Candles

The practice includes oil lamps and candles. Some people mistakenly believe that candles are dangerous, witchcraft, Voodoo, or Satanism. In this context, a candle is used only for prayer. Hoodoo has a lot to offer. There are many options for hoodoo scented candles. The most common candles are those in glass that include images of saints, angels, and angels in the back and front.

Hoodoo candle usage is quite simple. Use a candle with a color that corresponds to a particular need. For example, black candles for repelling insects and a green candle for money. It is then given the right dressing oil such as money drawing or money oil.

As you recite the right Psalm or Statement of Intent, the final step is lighting the candles. Hoodoo candles come with a range of colors. Some only have one color, while others have multiple colors. Others are more specific, like the Lucky lotto candle. Each candle has its own unique effect. Some candles come in human form. Other candles have skull- or penis-shaped shapes. Some candles possess sympathetic magic. The principle behind sympathetic magic says that like attracts. You can make a candle that represents what you need. Penis candles are available if you need to cast a spell for fertility.

These seven-day candles are illustrated below.

White can be used to gain guidance from the spirit or clarity. On Monday, you can use the white candles. You should use them before any work.

Blue candles are good for soothing the spirit as well as to guide it. It is best to use it Monday through Thursday.

The healing properties of green candles can be used to bring prosperity, money, health, wealth and luck. It can be used in firm statements.

Red candles are symbolic of love, courage and anger. You can use it Saturday and Tuesday.

Purple is used to invoke royalty feelings. It is best to use it on Thursdays and Saturdays for the best results.

Pink can be used to express your love for yourself, or to love other people more. It can be used every day.

You can use orange to bring about success in court cases. You can use it Sundays.

Yellow promotes laughter, communication, and energy, especially on Wednesdays or Sundays, for the best results.

Brown can help you solve your problem. You can use it anytime.

Before you start practicing this type magic, reflect on why. If Hoodoo is what you're after, and you want influence others with spells requiring sleight-of hand or influence to work, then you need to consider ethically whether this is possible.

African Ancestral Magic

Many Hoodoo practitioners today are African-Americans. However, many Hoodoo interpreters are non-black. The roots of the tradition can still be found in Central or West African mythology, which was brought to the United States during times of slavery.

Hoodoo has ancestor deification, which is also possible in some forms. Hoodoo is not an idolater practice. However, Hoodoo has many interpreters who are Christians. They also use the Spirituals for base magic.

African American folkmagic is meant to help you tap into supernatural forces that can improve your daily life.

Hoodoo is in a serious simplified manner the joining of three fantastic traditional strands magic, healing and folklore.

Voodoo is a religion based in the spiritual. It was originated in Africa and imported to Haiti by slave trade ships. Voodoo, which has a whole hierarchy system, can without doubt be described as a mystery faith in which not even its adherents truly know its origin.

Native American Herbal Knowledge.

A number of European spellbooks and other texts contained the set of magic skills and wisdom.

Hoodoo includes many Voodoo skills, but only when it concerns magic. While a single practitioner may take on students for hoodoo, conjure or rootwork, they are clearly not hierarchical.

So where is Hoodoo?

First, let's look at the historical context to help answer that question. Voodoo was first sent from Africa and Haiti to America. Then, on January 1, 2008, Haiti became an independent country called the Black Republic. Its lords and owners were expelled from the land. Many settlers arrived at New Orleans and took their domestic slaves and family members with them.

These blacks, enslaved from the Colony of Haiti by white men, had the seeds of Haitian Voodoo. They also syncretized a bit of Christianity they received while in slavery.

Slave workers in New Orleans and elsewhere in South America came into contact and eventually drank the healing techniques of the Indians. As they couldn't afford to pay for a physician, the only thing they had was their clothes. Yes, it was its property. To cure the disease, it would need a miracle or free treatment. In general, these formulas were provided by the Indians.

When the system for freedom began to take effect, few of these blacks became free. But many of their descendants learnt to read. The Grimoires provided them with tracts and books about Ceremonial Magic. This was complicated and extremely expensive. Also, practicing this kind of magic was not feasible. So they took in the best of it all, and little by little the Hoodoo culture was born.

Hoodoo, an obscure tradition, is more than 300 years old. It is still practiced by minorities. Although the history of Hoodoo is filled with sorrow, tears, blood, sweat, and sadness, it remains a beautiful practice that is rich in culture.

CONJURING HOOOO

How to conjure a hoodoo

It is important not to confuse hoodoo (magician) with hoodoo. Vodun, an older West African religion that teaches magick, is what gives rise to the term magician. It's a complex intertwining and interplay of magic, herbal remedies and tradition. It may also be called "root-working" or "root doctorsing" at times. You might have heard it described in blues music. Outsiders are often amazed by the mysterious hoodoo solemnities.

Mojo bags

Mojo bags, sometimes referred as prayer bag, originate from Africa. West Africa is the place where charm sacks are commonly used to attract suckers, drive down evil, and bring good luck. Red blarney forms the heart of most mojo bags. You can find bags made from green blarney to attract plutocrats as well as bags made of white blarney for baby blessings.

The contents vary according to the stoner's pretensions. It can contain roots, plants, sauces, beast corridors, minerals and commemoratives. The contents of a bag designed for someone with special needs is often similar to hair and nails. The more specific items they contain, then the more power they hold.

The bag must be "locked in place" to make it function. The bag should not be visible in order to make it work. Men will often conceal the bag by hiding it in their pants. Women use their bras more often than men.

Black cat bones

Black pussycats often are considered to be a bad auspice. A black catbone is still one the most important charms of a hoodoo. There's a belief that the bones can grant you invisibility, restore lost suckers, or give fame.

According to popular belief, black cats can bring bad luck.

Many believe that black cats bring bad luck. They have been discriminated because of this belief.

This is a myth that has existed for a long time. In many cultures, cats were thought to be positive. However witchcraft persecution made them lose popularity. Their deaths were a mass occurrence, but the truth is that it was the rodents spreading the disease that killed them and the cats that helped hunt.

Not only were women killed at the stake because they were accused of witchcraft but cats too were subject to persecution. They were charged with having links to witches. These women were later accused in the history of changing into these animals. This was why seeing a black kitten was like seeing a witch. Older women were the ones who found them and took care of them, which was later alleged to be witchcraft.

Four ginger stealer

Four stealers ginger is widely used in hoodoo. It is used to cover people, resolve complaints, keep undesirable people away, and remove curses.

Legend says the form dates back to Middle Periods-era thieves. The thieves were known for their habit of stealing Black Death victims. After they were arrested, they confessed that the pest four thieves ginger they had escaped from them weren't theirs. The recipe, also known as Marseille ginger or ginger ale, varies between manufacturers.

There are two classes.

They can be used for internal or external purposes. The result can include any combination of sauces. The majority of fashions still require at least four pieces of bone to be included in each pincher.

Goofer Dust

Goofer powder is a magical potion that's made from graveyard dirt. It also contains colorful complements that are similar to swabs and snakeskin. Kufua, which is a Bantu word that means "to go to death", gives the name. It can be used to curse, or to hurt someone. To guard against similar attacks, the Goofer Bag is always worn.

Goofer Dust is often spread along a victim's path. It can also be applied or used beneath their pillow or person. These symptoms almost mirror the complications of diabetes.

History reveals that Gregory Cucchiara (Queens New York) was sentenced to 50 years imprisonment in February 2016 for the murders of his parents. He decided to represent hisself after firing four defense attorneys. After representing himself he claimed his parents were deceased as a direct result of the hexagon with incense.

John the Conqueror Root

These come in three forms: high, lower, and John biting. Often, the original vacuity determines which variety of it is used. Biting John is an example of a gusto family member, which was used to manage abdominal pain and to influence legal opinions. Low John is usually made with Trillium wildflowerroots. High John is made from the woody stem of morning glory. After drying, it looks like the testicles in a dark-bearded men's genitals. John is used frequently in sexual spells. You will be able overcome any obstacles that come your way if you keep it with. It attracts plutocrats by being carried in green bags. If combined with a cinch, it can attract any kind of nut. John the Conqueror Root has been praised by players for his ability of bringing luck.

Footmark magic

Hoodoo has deep roots in footmark spells. It's all about throwing greasepaint in the path of a specific person. There are two main styles: placing jewels in a predetermined configuration in your opponent's path and putting dirt from the footmark in an empty bottle. There are many options. One is to mix some goo Arabic with hemp rope and pulverized iron and sprinkle them along your victim's route. You can ensure death by placing a combination cemetery smut or revealed snakeskin in the victim's path. Sometimes socks, shoes (or toenail pieces), or the bottom skin of victims are combined with magical maquillages. This old hoodoo trend is referenced in Robert Johnson's piece, Monuments in My Passway.

Bottle trees

Bottle trees appeared in the west African region of Congo in the ninth-century. They transported African slaves across the Atlantic to Europe and America. However, spirits can easily burn if exposed to sunlight in the morning. Bottle trees have been believed to bring good luck and rain. They also contribute enormously to the trees' blooming.

Bottles of any colour are accepted. But, Hoodoo prefers bottles that have a blue color. This is because it helps reflect both the sky & the water. Also, it acts as an inter-section between heaven & earth as well the living / the dead.

Bottle trees are found throughout southern Appalachia and the southern colony. However, their original meaning has been lost in many areas. These are more commonly used in hoodoos than for home fabrics and were made by tradesmen.

Cemetery smut

The graveyard dirt is a powerful tool for effective magic, as can be seen in the history of the Bokongo People of central Africa. However, dirt from a tomb cannot be taken without being purchased. This means you must connect with the deceased to offer them commodities in exchange for the often alcoholic taste they have for the earth and other commodities. Love spells are elegantly applied to the smuts that have been loved by you, and they are done with an immaculate, heartfelt manner. If wrong is what you want, a killer's burial is the best option. Scammers or hawkers can use the soil to create clutter and confusion.

Jack balls

This could be described as a collection magic objects wrapped in string. There is usually enough string left over to allow them to be hung. Jack balls were first made as Congo charms. They had certain numbers of knots that connected them to the amulets.

Jack balls are said bring luck or plutocrat. Some are used as augury. They are typically hung like pendulums to determine the direction. They can also be spun fast to produce a narcotic affect. Jack balls must be fed consistently to remain effective, similar to mojo bags.

The more precise the details at its core, the more power and influence the ball has.

Holy Bible

The bible is Hoodoo's greatest book. Most interpreters are Christians. Hoodoo traditions and the Christian south have intertwined.

The Bible is not just a resource for prayer; it can also serve as an amulet. Hoodoo's most recognizable part of Bible are the Spirituals.

Hoodoo doesn't mean that only the Bible is magical. Many Protestants believe in the ability of the verses and their power to heal physical and mental ailments.

Magician is associated with creepy, or spoken magic. These rituals and magic words are often performed in the middle-of-the-night. The history of West Africa is rooted in magic and it made its way to America through the slave trade. It was especially rehearsed here in Louisiana. Most people think of magicians as small black-magic dolls or those who are mistreated with needles. In reality, however, a magician can do much more.

Hoodoo Mountain Magic

Hoodoo in some parts the United States refers to mountain magical. Folk magical practices that are based in the southeastern United States frequently incorporate spells, foreshadowings or phylacteries. This is a wonderful example of how a magical, diasporic practice can become trans-artistic.

Despite the confusion common in people who don't know how to interpret magic, Hoodoo, Voodoo, or Vodoun are not the identical thing. The magician refers only to a select group of spirits and gods. This is true religion.

Harry Middleton Hyatt from Anglican was a minister and an Anglican mythologist who traveled to the American Southeast to interview Hoodoo people. His extraordinary collection of thousands if spells, interviews, and magical beliefs has been published.

Hyatt's weight has been question by scholars. His interviews with hundreds African Americans have also raised questions about his work. Hyatt appears to have no idea of Hoodoo's workings in the context of black culture. A lot of Hyatt's work is recorded on cylinders. It was also phonetically restated, giving it the appearance that he conceptualized the African-American Indian cants. Anyhow, with these issues in mind, the Hyatt volumes, simply named Hoodoo-Conjuration-Witchcraft-Rootwork are worth exploring for anyone interested in the practice of Hoodoo.

Magician, a religion. Magician is a religion originating in Africa that uses magic to achieve its goals. Its sanctuary for divinities, the Loans is equipped with scales, emblems power, tabernacles as well as observances. All of this, though, isn't yet planted in Hoodoo.

Hoodoo has its essence in the pursuit for fleshly benefits

Through magic.

Hoodoo's philosophy is that the end always justifies its means. There are no group observances because rituals have a unique imprint. The relationship with the Spirits, other than when he is passing on his knowledge or when the ritual demands additional actors, is intimate and private. Hoodoo originated out of Africa, and it has spread significantly in America, especially the New Orleans area. Marie Laveau is perhaps its most well-known proponent. This form of magic was created in Africa. But, it developed more rapidly than any other after slavery in America. Interpreters are known as "Conjuremen", or "Root Doctors".

The Bible is the most used book. Spirituals, in particular, are often used to help support spells. Because the ancient prayers contain a driving force that gives them uncommon magic powers, it is no surprise that they are so well-known. The sixth and seven books of Moses are also truely valid. They are grimoires that were written in the Renaissance, especially for seals. Conjureman can safely perform rituals with a kitchen grazed by spices, a piece or cloth, a little dirt, an infusion palette, many candles, and even a Bible, as opposed the western magician.

Hoodoo uses sauces. Prayers. Maquillages. Bags. Monuments. Cloth dolls. Beast remains. Colorful objects. It is common for the constituents to be replaced with others. Indeed, the Guru can also decide on the boluses. The origins and traditions of the different canvases or potions can affect how they look.

Simply put, the hoodoo can be described as folk magic used in Africa and America around the Mississippi. How can you define Hoodoo? Hoodoo is composed of many parts. Folk magic practices are the largest part and therefore most extensive of Hoodoo. These include those from Africa and around Mississippi. On the other side, it focuses on the intricate knowledge of magical workings in various plants, minerals, substances in the contexts hoodoo. A small portion of folk magic is used in the European region. The rootworker is a person who uses herbs and other substances as magic tools and who is guided and supported by the spirits of their spirit. The rootworker is sometimes called a two-headed man or woman because the spirit often "borrows her head" during magical work. Voodoo suggests that he is "ridden" by his spirit.

Anybody who works professionally within hoodoo with the necessary experience and qualifications is called a "hoodoo doctor", man or woman.

It is not clear where the origin of "Hoodoo", as it is called, is. According to some, "hoodoo", derives its name from "voodoo". However, this seems extremely unlikely. Hoodoo can be described as a magical folk belief. It was originated in Central Africa. The misunderstanding arises because whites commonly understand hoodoo as "voodoo", so they still confuse hoodoo in the wrong way. This is evident in New Orleans.

Hoodoo can be referred to in European terms as "witchcraft" and refers to both harmful spells or healing spells. In black communities, however this term is most commonly used to describe destructive spells.

Hoodoo actually covers everything from protection spells to love spells to money magic to the drawing off luck.

Simply put, there's four categories within hoodoo practioners:

Hoodoo Spiritual Doc: He is an ordained spiritual doctor who works to end magically-caused illnesses by prayer and magical assistance.

Hoodoo Healer, a natural healer that treats common ailments in the same way as a doctor.

Hoodoo Fortuneteller, a psychic who sees the future, can locate lost objects, and can help one find what's needed to move forward in their spiritual lives.

Rootworker. Uses herbs and substances for magical purposes. His spirits guide and support him.

Hoodoo: American-African folk magical art

The emphasis is always put on one's personal magical power. Hoodoo isn't a hierarchical system. There aren't priests or other levels between practitioners and laity.

If a hoodoo specialist accepts a new student, he will then initiate him into his individual ritual practice. This may be different than that of other practitioners. Hoodoo is a living practice. While there are some rules to follow, each spell has its own set of rules. You will never stop learning. There is no finish, no stage at which you can reach the final stage. There are no magical degrees or initiations. Just perpetual learning.

The hoodoo of working with the Haitian Vodou religion's loss or other spirits is nothing new.

This work is, however, reserved for the rootworker. He works with his personal spirit and won't ask for assistance from any other spirits. This is done for respect for foreign spirit, on the contrary, it's also for his self-protection.

Like many folk magic practices and hoodoos, it uses the magical power from herbs, roots, animals components (e.g. bones), as well as body materials (hair and nails, etc. spirit, and other materials. In the Hoodoo, there are many magic tools, including B. Hoodoo oil, magic powders. gris-griss. incenses. magic salts and ritual candles. Many of these magic techniques are also found in African or Afro-Caribbean religious traditions, including Santeria, Candomble, Mayombe, Santeria, and Loans. You can make "tricks", use rituals such as candle magic, spell baths, magic candles, spiritual house cleaning, drive out "evil spirits", cast various spells or their counterspells. Lucky pouches and amulets are also available. The list can be extended at will. In the Hoodoo, dreams are also important as the spirits may report through dreams to give the rootworker some tips.

Hoodoo does not represent the truth

Hoodoo cannot be considered a religion. Hoodoo has nothing to do with Vodou. Vodou refers to a religion. Voodoo's name is derived from an African word. It can also be translated as "Spirit", and "God". English-speaking Christian missionaries in the 19th and 20th centuries equated the term Hoodoo to the Vodou religion. This motto, which sounds almost identical, is most likely the same. This is particularly true for beginners in Vodou or Hoodoo. People interested in African folk magical techniques often believe that they must learn Voodoo to make it work magic, but are not interested in any religion. Loa des Vodou is a religious organization that seeks to fulfill religious needs.

Before you devote your life to Vodou or hoodoo magic you need to decide which path to follow. Both approaches sound alike, but they are fundamentally very different. For a rootworker, however, they can both be mixed.

Hoodoo in practice

The hoodoo simply means folk magic. It is made up different parts. It is composed of several parts. The largest part, and the most complex, consists of rituals, methods of application. They are practiced in Africa around the Mississippi. But, there are also folk magic applications in European areas.

It is important to have a solid understanding of the magical powers of plants, minerals and other substances. People who practice and follow this kind of magic are called root workers.

Hoodoo uses the knowledge of magical and healing properties of plants, minerals and animal components. Folk magic is often used in everyday life, even if it is not obvious.

So, depending on what the hoodoo practitioners has learned, he might also incorporate this knowledge in his practice.

What do you do for magic in a Hoodoo?

It depends on the problem. Although the list might never be complete, we are just listing what can "conjured" to solve the problem.

These spells might sound strange, similar to matching hoodoos oils, whose name is usually the same as the matching magic.

This simply ensures that the supply is secure. The most important part, however, is the money. We all know it: the good money. But very few people are able to get enough of it to lead a peaceful life.

The magic is all around us:

To get a quick buck.

To get a raise.

Someone who forgives or forgets your debts

To make a good impression in order to get a better position.

To have a steady stream of money.

To have enough food to eat.

Next are love, sex (weddings), and children. These are all areas that cannot easily be ignored and can offer enough energy in daily life. There are many great spells available.

Make yourself irresistible

Spell for fiery passion

You must get him/her telling the truth.

You can ask him/her for a marriage.

So the divorce can go well.

Magic against loversickness

Make your mother love you.

Children need to be well behaved in public.

Conjure your ex back.

It's magic to get through the baby-nights as mom or dad.

Increase the love and loyalty of your partners and so on.

Third is spiritual cleansing, and home. These are capitalized under the hoodoo. Those who fail to purify their spiritual lives bring back the worst things that can be found in their homes and cause them grief, anger, stress and more. It is essential that you clean your house regularly and do the same for yourself. Today, stress is a major issue.

The following spells may be assigned:

Find the perfect apartment, great house.

Spiritual hoodoo home cleaning

Spiritual cleansing.

Driveaway guests that don't want the opportunity to leave.

Driveaway ghosts. Ghosts and the paranormal.

Driveaway bad neighbors.

Sell your house quickly.

Harmonize your relationship with family members

Fourth, you can use magic to overcome general difficulties

Stop smoking.

Let go of old habits and ways.

You can get a liar or a fraudster to tell the truth.

Silence blasphemers.

Forbidding bullying

Protect your family members, yourself, your pets, or your car.

Be healthy in times of crisis

Ask for healing

You can drive a stalker away.

A friend can make an enemy your friend.

Change people.

Get in touch.

It's a spell of nightmares.

So you have plenty of reasons for being magical.

Is hoodoo a form of voodoo?

Even though some people may believe it, it isn't true. Voodoo/Vodou (at least one of its lineages) is an West African religion that was brought from West Africa to Haiti by slaves. Hoodoo can be described as a magical folk belief.

Voodoo means religion and Hoodoo means folk magic.

How can I integrate hoodoo within my daily life?

First, be open to seeing the signs of trouble in your life. You don't need to do hoodoo when everything is going well. If everything is going well, you don't have to be magical.

You should identify the areas you want to improve. Your problem cannot be solved if you don't have sobriety. We suggest that you consider a Hoodoo case study, which focuses on these very issues.

Once you understand your problem, you will first try to solve the problem in a worldly fashion. Sometimes the solution is right at your fingertips. When you've tried everything else, magic will happen. Example: If your partner leaves you, you want them back.

Hoodoo: The best method.

1. You should think objectively and with sobriety about what you've done to him.

2. You are able to try to talk with him and to build a relationship through conversations.

3. If he blocks your view, you may wonder if it is really right for him.

4. You can be magical if you see him as the right person in your eyes.

In our example, the spells would be cast in the following order:

1. Grounding and spiritual cleaning can stabilize your psyche.

2. Reflection magic can help you discover what it is that you truly want.

3. You can use cleansing spells and other magic to dispel negative energies. (Owning and spiritual house cleaning)

4. Magic to enhance your charm and to make you irresistible

5. Come to my magic.

Can anyone do hoodoo

Yes. If your heart beats fervently for magic and you cannot envision a life without magic. If you are open-minded to learning, and if practical sobriety is your goal.

Hoodoo isn't for those who are esoteric. This isn't about fancy flourishes and a "I'm better than you" mentality. It's about the real problems that need solving.

Does hoodoo really work all the time?

No. It is not true. Anyone who claims their hoodoo magic does 100 places every time is lying. Hoodoo can't be a wish-fulfilling magic that does everything. It's not so easy. Because we are dealing directly with the world and the fates you wish to change. Hoodoo spells create the potential for "destiny" to be changed or steered in a different direction. It is like an automobile following the track. The motorist will only be able to drive on the marked track. He has the ability to choose his destination but must remain on the specific thruway. On the way, he'll pass colorful destined stations.

A hoodoo motorcyclist sees a business jam or other problems on a specified motorway. He uses his knowledge, magic, and other means to get off the motorway. Sometimes these new paths appear only by the magic of God.

How can I learn how to hoodoo

If you come from a magic family, you will be able to take the base with your and expand. But, your gift, will, hard work, and talent will determine whether or not your spells are successful. Find out about medicinal shops.

Learn magic tricks (sigil magic), ritual magic, and more. To be more sane, expand your perception. Because you cannot be in your own senses if you prefer an illusionist world to reality.

Hoodoo (or magic) is a form used by the African American populace in the southern U.S. This type can also be known as conjure. This refers to the combination of many cultures and traditions that were brought from Africa.

Hoodoo contains traditional practices from different religions. These include African traditional religious practices and the practices of American native peoples. American English is the first to document hood in 1875. It can be used as a noun or transitive verb. AAVE sometimes uses it as a noun to describe a spell. However, it could also be used as an adjectival to describe a practitioner. Hoodoo may also be known by its regional synonyms invocation and evoke.

They are not all synonyms. In particular, Witchcraft is problematic as a synonym in the sense it might imply a negative moral assessment on Hoodoo practice. Or it could be confused or misunderstood with the contemporary Wiccan religion.

It is important to remember that a hoodoo doctors should not be regarded as a rootworker.

Hoodoo has little to do Voodoo. (Voodoo) is an African-American magical and spiritual practice. It was developed by kidnapped West African African slaves. The practice combines some elements of Judaism with Christianity. Everything suggests that Hoodoo's birthplace is the Mississippi River delta. This area has the highest concentration of slaves and it travels to Cuba, Haiti, Jamaica, and other countries. It was mistakenly called the Voodoo.

Hoodoo is, in theory, an attempt alter concrete reality to the benefit of its practitioners. This is not different from any other spiritual or occult tradition. Hoodoo has one thing that sets it apart from other magical traditions: It demands absolute surrender from all its acolytes. The Hoodoo demands absolute surrender in order to perform its rites.

Hoodoo thought was greatly influenced by Christianity. African slaves adopted the belief that God, as the biblical God, rewards and punishes its children. This idea was adapted to their ethical system, which is often called "barbarian". However, they never thought of slavery as food for their native villages.

Slavery was something that African slaves would admit to on their land. This was true in certain cases. However, the comparison ends there. A fist strike is both violent and bombing. The volume of violence they unleash is unmatched.

However, Hoodoo did accept the idea of curses. Why would I do that to you? If the God for the Whites punishes and rewards fairly, the only effective curse would be one that is performed with divine approval.

Hoodoo's roots had strong impact from the exodus account. Moses functions as both a military and spiritual leader. He also acts as a magician and "channels divine justice", to punish Pharaoh's troops, and benefit slaves searching for freedom. Hoodoo believes Moses is just a conductor. Hoodoo Wizard also operates on the same principle, but on a smaller level.

A curse, incantation, and enchantment are of no real value, nor can they exist without divine guidance. It's no surprise that the Hoodoo book of spells & spells is precisely the Bible, especially The Old Testament. Hoodoo membership is initiated by reading Psalms.

Hoodoo's main purpose is to obtain the primary energies of nature. This is for us to see, and to give them to those who do their rites. This search often serves immediate purposes, such as fortune, love or revenge, health or power.

Hoodoo seeks intermediaries who will help him connect with God. In this case, Hoodoo summons the spirit of his ancestors and asks them to intercede on behalf of his followers.

Hoodoo books are rare in that they accurately describe the history of this culture. Instead, these essays are often anthropological essays that rarely venture beyond their scope of action. There are only a few Hoodoo books that can be cited. These include Harry Middleton Hyatt's The Hoodoo Conjuration. Also, in fiction, Mumbo Jumbo (Mumbo Jumbo), Ishmael River Reed. El dia de Mama, by Gloria Naylor. Hoodoo causes unusual paranormal phenomenon. Charles W. Chesnutt's The Sorceress (The Conjure Woman), which uses Hoodoo as a catalyst for primordial forces to remain in constant tension.

The Hoodoo.

Blues derives its origins from the blues songs that slaves sung in the cotton-fields. Also called "field hollers", they entertained workers and managed the rhythm of work.

The 17th century saw the transfer of slaves from Africa to America.

The European conquerors were the ones that introduced the Catholic religion to Louisiana or New Orleans. The slaveowners tried to force their religion onto the slaves, and anyone caught practicing their beliefs would be put to death. So the slaves "disguised" their religion and made it conform to the regional one. Thus, they achieved a mixture hoodoo and Catholicism.

But what exactly does Hoodoo mean?

Hoodoo is a form folk magic and spiritual practice that originates from African-American culture. Hoodoo does not refer to religion. It is an expression of spirituality that uses "spells" to help with security issues.

Hoodoo can be described as a traditional form magic. The meanings of the term Hoodoo will vary depending on its wearer and those who are practicing it. Hoodoo is believed to be the origin of rootwork and folk magic.

The practice of Hoodoo is popularized by African Americans. However, many other non-black practitioners also follow the practice. This tradition and practice have roots in West African folk culture and were brought to America during times of slavery.

It was common for people to be confused about the different types of magic, Voodoo or Vodoun (Vodoun). Voodoo (Vodoun) can be described a complete religion which draws a specific group of deities. Hoodoo however, can be described a set folk magic skills. Hoodoo is a form of magic that can be traced back at least to early African magic.

Harry Middleton Hyatt from Anglican was a minister and folklorist. He traveled throughout the United States interviewing Hoodoo practitioners. He collected an impressive and extensive collection of thousands, including magical beliefs and practices. His interviews were then combined into multiple volumes.

Tarot of the Hoodoo.

This divination method and guide cards is based upon the American Hoodoo tradition. These exchanges produced a multicultural population and a wealth of knowledge, known as Hoodoo or Rootwork.

Hoodoo Tarot, which celebrates American rootswork's complex legacy, combines Hoodoo's esoteric botanical knowledge with Tarot divination. Each card of the 78 is laid out as a traditional Tarot deck. Katelan Foisy has created full-color paintings that capture classic

Tarot imagery. Tayannah Lee McQuillan provides a brief history of Hoodoo. The guide also includes information about its many influences, which include European influences as well African and Native American roots. She explores traditional divination techniques used by rootworkers, including fortune-telling, and explains how Hoodoo and Tarot can be combined. McQuillan offers a comprehensive explanation of the meanings of each Major Arcana card, and all four Minor Arcana suits (suits. baskets. needles..), which are based on Hoodoo history and Tarot. She tells about the rootworker or symbol featured, as well as magical plants associated with them and a pertinent bibliography.

HISTORY HOODOO

Hoodoo was a mix of spiritual practices from North America and African slaves. It is kept confidential. Hoodoo was a mixture African traditions with Western persuasions. It spread to America after the Great Migration. Its frequency of rehearsals will vary depending on the location and the dispositions of its owners.

Gullahs at the east coast had relative freedom and insulation that allowed them preserve traditional West African cultural practices. The magic bags (also known as "Magic Bags") were used to resist slavery. William Webb ordered the slaves should find some roots and put them into their bags.

Haitian influence

Zora Neale Hurston a hoodoo-generator and an African-American artist anthropologist reports in her essay Hoodoo in America. She says that witchery was most prominent along the Gulf Coast. African Haitians brought conjuring techniques with them. They were modified by European artistic influences comparable to Catholicism. Some Haitian Vodou techniques were retained; others created their own Hoodoo.

Hoodoo can be used in mobility for black people who have moved from the pastoral South to other areas of the north. African American communities saw white druggists open stores, and they began to take care of the details that their guests wanted and also those that they had.

A grimoire is one of the seven books written by Moses. While Moses is believed to have written it, the oldest manuscripts date from the middle of 19th century. Here are some examples of its importance in hoodoo to interpreters:

Hoodoo spread all over the United States, when African Americans left Delta during Great Migration and Fortunetelling

There are several types of augury that have been used in hoodoo.

Cleromance

Includes casting small objects (similar to bones, bones or stems, coins, nuts and monuments, cells or sticks, etc.).

Kartman

Fortune telling using practitioner cards.

Natural and forensic divination.

Studying the positions and movements heavenly bodies and their effects on nature and other matters.

Augury

The prediction of the future is often made by the foreshadowing of marvels.

Pyromancy

A form based on dreams.

Practices

In a process known "hunt", a hoodoo-guru will seek to liberate a person's spirit so that a Gullah religious can accept it. A form will start with singing and practicing a ring laugh. To praise the Christian God, they used canticles such the running canticles (or rings crying), despite their African singing style. Enslaved Africans were forced onto becoming Christians. They were given a mix Christian-African spiritual practices to learn, which helped shape the hoodoo. In the United States, some black churches still hold hoodoo rehearsals. The Gullah/ Geechees, who are trippers and Northern Preceptors, have been describing an African-looking ritual called "ring screaming", since the mid-19th Century. The Holy Spirit descends to crown the ring. "The ring screaming with hoodoo was born in the Congo Region of Africa. An example of a ring that shouts "Ring!" is an old form that follows the indirect patterns of the (Ba] Congo cosmogram. The cosmogram symbol is a representation of the energy flow that connects the spiritual to the physical worlds. Counterclockwise movement in a ring cry is meant to bring the spirit with the actors' chanting, supplicate, and singing. Rivals don't lift their feet from the ground while carrying the ring. A ring cry refers to a ritual with high spiritual mending rates. It is the same as transcendental vision search, astral protuberance and nirvana. "A ring cry must be performed by actors who are free from their brain presence. They should allow the spirit of the ring to rule and enter their bodies. This symbol follows the indirect patterns of the (Ba/Congo cosmogram. The symbol for the cosmogram shows the pattern that energy flows to connect the spiritual and the physical worlds. Counterclockwise movements in a ring cry are designed to bring the spirit with the actors' chanting, supplicate, or chant. Rivals don't lift their feet while carrying the ring. A ring cry refers to a ritual with high spiritual mending rates. They are as prevalent as transcendental visual searches, astral protuberance and nirvana. "A ring call must be made. Actors must release their brain presence to allow the spirit of the ring to rule. This symbol follows the indirect patterns of the (Ba] Congo cosmogram. The cosmogram symbol depicts the pattern that energy flows to connect the spiritual and material worlds. The counterclockwise movement in a ring cry brings the spirit to life as the actors chant supplicate, chant, and chant. Rivals don't lift their bases from the ground while they move the ring. "A ring cry refers to a ritual with high spiritual mending rates. They are as prevalent as transcendental visual searches, astral protuberance and nirvana. "A ring cry must be performed by actors who are free from their brain presence. it connects both the spiritual and physical realms. Counterclockwise movements, which are chants, supplicates, and chants, are designed to bring the spirit together during a "ring cry". Rivals don't lift their feet from the ground while they move the ring. "A Ring cry is a ritual involving spiritual mending rates. It can be as powerful as transcendental Vision Searches, astral Protuberance or Nirvana. "For a Ring cry to work, actors need to let go of their brain presence to allow the spirit to enter and rule the ring. it connects both the spiritual and physical realms. The counterclockwise movement, which is used during a "ring cry", is designed to bring out the spirit. As the actors chant, pray, and chant, it brings the spirit together. Rivals don't lift their bases from the ground while they move the ring. "A Ring cry is a ritual with a spiritual mending rate that is as prominent as transcendental Vision searches, astral Protuberance, or Nirvana. "A ring cry must be performed by actors who can let go of their brain presence in order to allow the spirit inside the ring to rule.

Spirit agreement

Hoodoo was meant to help people gain supernatural powers that would improve their lives. Hoodoo has been said to aid people in their quest for power ("luck") and negotiate in many areas of their lives, including love, career, finances, and the workplace. The intense use of sauces or minerals, along with the effects of an exist, is similar to many spiritual and medicinal folk traditions. The conjuring practice includes contact with ancestors. Moses is spiritually affected by the enumeration, or naming, of spirituals. Interpreters of Hoodoo magic often have an analogous understanding to Moses' biblical figure. It is clear that there are obvious parallels between Moses (and metaphysical influence similar to magic) and the biblical accounts detailing his battle with Pharaoh. Moses is able to perform magic tricks or magical warnings, like turning his staff into one. Yet, his greatest heartbreak was in using his powers to free Hebrews from slavery.

Bible as an amulet

Hoodoo states, "Everyone believes that the Bible the great magic books of the world." It serves many functions for the guru, including a source to spells. This is especially true given the importance of the book Secrets of the Spirituals to hoodoo cultures. This book gives instructions on how to use spirituals to create effects such a safe trip, headaches, or marital connections. The Bible isn't only a spiritual resource, but it can also be used as a suggestion amulet. It can be used to "bring the crossroad", or worn openly on certain sides, while facing particular directions.

Ghosts

One belief is that although one's soul goes to God after death it may still be with us. Ghosts can be used to bring good luck and bad deeds to the world. You can also summon spirits to heal or kill others and prognose the future.

Magician Persuasions and Differences

Vodun Folkway has a simpler and more commonly used spiritual practice that Hoodoo Vodun's. It is being practiced across West Africa, in countries like Togo, Benin and Burkina Faso. . American Vodoun Loa is deified. Vodun is closely linked to the Vodou, Louisiana's magician and the Vudu, Dominican Republic. Archaeologists located hoodoo vestiges among

Maryland's slave colonies. They proved that West African practices were deeply ingrained in the United States thanks to African slaves. . Archaeologists located vestiges that revealed a mixture between West African spiritual practices as well as Christian spiritualities among slaves in another colony in Maryland. . This was Ezekial's Bible-derived wheel. It mixed with Central African Congo's Cosmogram. In black Americans' hoodoo ritual, the Congo Cosmogram is shown. Inventing complexion pots from enslaved Africans in a South Carolina former slave colony, archaeologists used the Congo cosmogram to create them.

Colono earthenware ceramic coliseums from South Carolina, which were found in swash tops and slave-diggings sites in South Carolina, suggest that African American preachers used identical symbols of this macrocosm further back than one hundred and fifty centuries ago. The Congo Cosmogram in Hoodoo also has a physical representation called a Crossroad. Because of the maturity and faith of Africans who were brought out to Africa during the slave trading, there are many Congo religious beliefs and beliefs.

Spiritual force

Manual maquillages, mojo hands, canvases (van van canvas, dragon's blood, etc. Numerous pastoral Hoodoos use amulets and a variety of other items as their base. However, some companies have been able to offer colorful hoodoo products for civic and civic interpretations. These are sometimes called spiritual inventories. Many patent drugs and cosmetics as well menage cleaning products are targeted at mainstream consumers. There are products that can be used both as traditional and spiritual inventories. These include the Four Stealers Ginger (or Florida Water), and Red Devil Lye.

Cosmology

In Hoodoo studies there was a Christian influence. Traditional West African study believed that equilibrium was the key to all mortal trials. "Various African spiritual traditions revered a unisex supreme Being who created the whole world and wasn't preoccupied in the affairs human beings. To solve mortal problems, minor bone Spirits were invoked.

Zora said Nealehurston about this matter. According to Zora, Hoodoo was founded there. Six days were spent casting spells and learning important words. The world below was also created. "From this perspective the biblical numbers are often recast. Hoodoo Doctors and the Bible both can be used for spells and as defensive amulets. The Christian Bible contains many ideas that can be combined to make the belief more acceptable.

Moses as a magician

Hoodoos often interpret the biblical Moses in an analogous way. Egregious parallels in Moses and intentional metaphysical influence (similarly to magic) are evident in the biblical accounts regarding Moses' battle against Egypt. Moses is able to perform magic tricks or magical warnings, like turning his staff into one.

Yet, his greatest heartbreak was in using his powers to free Hebrews from slavery.

AUTHOR/GROUP HISTORY

hoodoo had no clear origin. The first written mentions to hoodoo came in a Natchez, Mississippi review in 1849. All other references to the term concentrated on the Mississippi River Valley late XNUMX.

Hoodoo has a mysterious origin, but was popular in the early years of 2008 as a term for African diasporic magicalism.

In social North America, and eventually in America, vibrant African traditions intertwined and acclimated the rudiments from the Native American and European societies that they encountered. The practice of spearing juice from galangal roots on slaves to protect themselves against abuse began in west-central Africa. Magician worshipers in the Mississippi River Valley called on West African divinities to perform magic.

Their ministry includes fortune telling and casting spells that bring happiness, love, or the like. Numerous people claimed that they were able magically to harm and heal guests who had been harmed by their guests. Hoodoo-interpreters were also known to have created accouterments to assist slaves fleeing and to teach religionists how root and spiritual maquillages can be used to protect them from the cruelty of masters. Conjuration gained another dimension with the liberation of slaves. The purpose of phylacteries was to increase employment and the number of plutocrats. Instead of protecting themselves against the possessors and appointing hoodoo interlocutors to guard guests against the Jim Crow-period system of judicial review, which was notoriously toxic against African Americans being charged with crimes.

While the nineteenth century was over, hoodoo still existed. The lonely interpreters who gathered their accouterments naturally never lost their relevance, but they were in decline with spiritual force assimilation. Botanical forcehouses became a major source of vegetable curiosities. In turn, spiritual and occult writers were being less frequently sold to African Americans.

FAITH/DOCTRINES

The principle or contagion holds that things will influence each others when they come in contact. This principle is most obvious for items that contain materials linked to others that the manufacturer may wish to help.

Sometimes sympathy and contagion go hand in hand. To achieve this, you need a child's toy doll that portrays the sick person. In order to tie the disease to your doll in a sympathetic, contagious way, you should decorate the doll using ribbons.

According to some, these forces or beings were capable of instilling spiritual power. In this worldview the main distinction between an ordinary object and an amulet was that conjurers claimed the ability to control or alter the mind and classify the latter as good or poor based upon the goals of their clients and the sympathetic or contagious capabilities it contains.

PRACTICES / RITUALS

You might find a few hoodoo methods that are quite different. Healing curses, by contrast, follow a multi-level system. In the latter scenario, the conjurer would determine the source of the pain. The conjurer would end the healing by removing the curse from the victim's body, which allowed him to recover. In many situations, the conjuring practitioner reversed or spiritually administered the curse to the victim.

This is a wonderful example of the whole process. Hyatt's informant was called "witchcraft" after a doctor failed to help. The initial treatment of salting the wound and washing it with urine failed. The conjurer then informed the client that the pain was supernatural. It had been caused by a medium placed under the victim's bed. When the man returned home from work, he discovered a white bag containing five little balls sewn and fastened. After the victim had returned the bag, the hoodoo boy burned it. Although the conjurer declined to recast it on the victim, he did offer to instruct his client how to do it. The aggrieved party should put a piece of his chair into a half - gallon jar, and bury it in the path of an enemy. The man did it and later found out that the woman who injured him actually had a small cut to her ankle.

The practice of the Hoodoo was more focused on the person seeking to obtain supernatural help than the professional conjurer as spiritual supply businesses became more popular. In some situations, shop clerks served as conjurers. They would recommend certain roots, oils, incense, Bible verses and the process to use their power. Sometimes the nearest consumers would come to consult after reading a book, such as The Master's Book of Candle Burning or The Life and Work of Marie Lavender. Hoodoo has grown to be a self service activity for a greater number of people.

ORGANISATION/LEADERSHIP

Hoodoo does not have the same formal leaders that can persuade. Instead, mindfulness was based on the guru's success. In the 1800s, the relationship between conjurers with those who sought their help was akin to that between a professional or a customer. People seeking supernatural guidance sought out those they considered stylish and able to help them. The hoodoo-guru would provide guidance and/or spells for the purpose of achieving the desired results. (Right picture) Some experts would focus on one aspect of the process. Others might claim the ability to do all.

The interpreters were able to use their supposed supernatural powers in a variety of ways. Inductions were a common way to start in the Mississippi River Valley. Many believed that the ability supplicate was a gift or a curse from God. Signs were used to indicate the delegation of authority similar to that which was claimed. Another common way to acquire supernatural capabilities was through the process of heredity. One example is that spiritual strength was measured by the fact that one was born in Africa after liberation. A source of the miraculous gift was the descent from your immediate ancestors, who had supplicated. This is a widespread source, probably since the late 19th century but possibly even earlier.

Marie Laveau was the notorious New Orleans Voodoo priestess. It is believed that she has at least one descendant. Buzzard was a South Carolina hoodoo specialist who passed his practice on through his son-inlaw.

Before 2014, most hoodoo translators were African American. But with the advent spiritual force stores, an increasing number non-blacks became interested in this new retail version of hoodoo. Cracker Jack Drugstore was established in New Orleans by a white Belgian-American man. Many shopkeepers became Jewish emigrants and turned to dealing with hoodoo items to make ends work in an age when society considered them to be ignorant.

Latin American entrepreneurs, which are often businesses for Latin American interpreters, have been more in demand.

American persuasions like Santeria are now hoodoo and sham shops. New Orleans' F and F

Botanical and Candle Shop is an excellent example.

No matter their race, no matter if they served a professional-client base, or as a company that sells spiritual goods to customers, hoodoo interpretations are considered an economic occupation. For illustration, Marie Laveau. Even though she was not wealthy, it was enough for an African American of her time who had enough plutocrats to enjoy slaves. Caroline Dye (a well-known magician, from Newport, Arkansas) is reported to have failed an obese woman more than a generation ago (Wolf 1970). His practice helped him buy multitudinous grains, start a log company, and trade nags.

Hoodoo conferred power to interpreters in other ways, as well as the fiscal prices. Example: Hoodoo doctors with a track record of success gained influence over anyone who admired and stressed them. The most common effect of the conjurers was on the bondholders. Hoodoo could be used by many people, including Frederick Douglass and Henry Bibb (unborn anti-slavery champions), to prevent enslavement. Others sought supernatural help to control worldly areas that they felt would benefit their masters and the vagaries of happiness. Some others went above and beyond their particular influence. Gullah Jak, a hoodoo master and assistant from Denmark Vesey was an excellent example. Numerous conjurers also assisted with the leadership of uprisings in the colonizer, antebellum, and post-colonial periods. Additionally, literal reports indicate that whites valued the power of conjurers. This raised their expectations for these interpreters at a period when African Americans were in their prime. After their freedom, interpreters were important members of society. Samuel C. Taylor, a Tennessee conjurer, met a similar figure near Tuscumbia. Taylor decided not to assign the man any role, but he still considered him the most powerful person within this section.

PROBLEMS/CHALLENGES

In the past, legal repression was used against hoodoos and similar practices. In 1692, the first witch accused in Salem was a hoodoo-loving slave. Some slave owners tried eliminating hoodoo during the antebellum period as a source slave revolt and individual hostility. The summoners' arsenal included spells that kill, make sick, or harm and some slave riot leaders were even involved in African supernaturalism. New Orleans was the place where most of these oppressions were visible. New Orleans police often broke up illegal slave meetings and voodoo services. An 1820 article entitled "Idolatry and Quackery" documented the disruption at such a meeting. It was also mentioned in the first of numerous religious news items about the city.

The other whites, however, avoided confrontation due to their own fear of or admiration of the power and hoodoo practitioners. Gladys-Marie Fry states that some masters used supernaturalism as a way to control their relationship through fear.

Both African-Americans (whites) and blacks saw the Civil War merely as an epoch of a long-ago past, in the decades that followed it's end.

Appleton's Diary XNUMX carries a sample report titled Witchcraft Among the Negroes.

The White and religion have unsuccessfully fought this barbaric legacy.

Some pieces did more than criticize ideas. They pointed out other social evils in the pieces. Der Plantagen Neger a Freeman, for instance, saw hoodoo to be a power "to disrupt work" or "to disorganize the race societies." He also accused conjurers with poisoning.

This is where the repression was continued. While the antebellum rules banning slave gatherings were antiquated, they were still in place. As with Jim Crow America's other features, ethnic values were used to protect power in the hands the white mature. Hoodoo was targeted by law enforcement and well-meaning liberals in an attempt cover the public. One example: In 1891, a doctor supported efforts of the Florida Medical Association to stop what he called an "undisciplined sin" in which African American midwives were allowed to deliver babies. One reason he did this was because he was concerned about women's lives. He also said that many African American midwives were ignorant of their profession, as they relied on supernaturalism instead of wisdom.

Recent efforts to drive hoodoo away from American society are being criticized. To correct the errors of the history, recent notes on hoodoo helped his grasp and devalue his lower palatable features such as sickness spells and Death. Since 1930s, Harlem Renaissance writer Zora Neale Hurston's Hoodoo and Mules, many fabrication historians or pens have seen Hoodoo through the same lens. They consider conjuration a vital part of African American culture and something to be celebrated. Hurston's original contribution in fabrication was outstanding, even though he published "Hoodoo in America" as both a scientific magazine for scientists and Mules for the general public.

Alice Walker (Susheel Bibbs), Jewell Parker Rhodes (Judl Parker Rhodes), Arthur Flowers, Ishmael Reid, and Jewell Phillip Rhodes have all adopted the hoodoo-doc as a symbol African American freedom.

They are also the most important companions to wisdom. Katrina Hazzard Donald is a fine example.

The Old African American Hoodoo System - MojoWorkin'

Hoodoo can be interpreted in a positive or negative way, but it remains an integral part African American history and society. Although conjuration has lost its popularity, it's not going away.

This practice of religious worship, which originated in Africa, involves pleasing and praising spirits to receive love, money, and health.

Hoodoo vs Voodoo

Voodoo may be described as a religion which has two types, namely Louisiana Vodou in Haiti and Louisiana Vodoun in Louisiana. It is also an African folk magic and is widely practiced today in America.

Hoodoo was a blend of spiritual traditions and practices created by African slaves who migrated to North America. It is kept confidential. Hoodoo was a mixture African traditions with Western persuasions. It was popularized in the USA by the Great Migration. Its frequency of rehearsals will vary depending on its location and the disposition of its owner. Gullahs at the coast's east were given insulation and relative liberty that allowed them preserve traditional West African cultural practices. The magic bags (also known as "Magic Bags") were used to resist slavery. William Webb ordered the slaves should find some roots and place them inside.

Hoodoo is referred to in West Africa as "Ggbo" or African American folk magical. It consists primarily African folk beliefs and practice with a mixture of Native American and European botanical knowledge. The rituals are different depending on who is performing them. There is no single approach that one should follow. Some spells that are part of hoodoo may be used with biblical text. The majority of these texts can be found in the book called psalms.

This practice is intended to enable people to harness supernatural forces to improve the quality of their daily lives. Voodoo was named after an African word, which means "god" (or "spirit") in African.

The History of Blues. Blues. Hoodoo. Mojo.

The influence of Christianity on African American slaves was profound, but the religion did not neglect to preserve some of Africa's animistic traditions. The slave route, which ran from West Africa through the ports in West Indies to North America, was instrumental in the formation of Afro-Caribbean cultures. These cultures would then migrate to North America and continue to instill the North American Blues, which is the core of hoodoo. In a sense the hoodoo may be considered the religion in the blues, while the blues can be considered the hymn of hoodoo.

From the very beginning, African religions had been dismissed by the white men, who treated them as superstitions that were only a part of their "childish" black minds. The ban on the religion of Africans in many areas of the country was implemented during the first half the eighteenth centuries. Acts of witchcraft or whipping were often punished. Most of the North American slave Africans were subject to the Anglo American Protestant Christian hegemony and had no relationship with their African spiritual systems.

One of the few North American exceptions where African slaves could follow non-Protestant faiths such as Catholicism, Louisiana, or the Northeast Quaker faith, is the practice hoodoo.

The hoodoo is lacking the essential elements that make up any religion. This includes hierarchical leaders and places of worship as well as defined deities. The hoodoo could be considered more than a religious system. It is a fragmented form of magic and medicine that is highly individualized. It addresses the main themes of love, life, health and prosperity. Although it was born in Africa, the hoodoo still believes that all objects as well as dreams and signs have their own vital energy. The only thing required to get the desired results from hoodoo is to be able direct those energies.

Medicine and magic can transform the world and be used in both healing and harmonizing ways. It's no surprise that this ability is associated both with the hoodoo with devil and the blues as his music. Ma Rainey's Black Dust Blues offers a good example for hoodoo in blues as a causative agents of disease. A jealous woman accuses another man of taking her property and vows revenge. However, when the victim arrives home to find black dust all over his driveway, he is then struck with the disease. In the lyrics it is noted how, even though revenge is the theme, the use of hoodoo to counteract socially ineligible behaviors is also highlighted. The whole hoodoo works as a social, spiritual, and law enforcement tool. The blues can be your informant.

The blues have a lot of lyrics that talk about a desire for or need to travel. Traveling is an act of transformation. Mojo is a Kilongo word that means "spiritual spirit", "strength", or "soul".

The mojo, which is used to initiate transformation in blues music, allows both the performer or his audience to connect with the supernatural. The phrase "Leaving this Morning" can be heard in many blues songs. However, it's not just a message about a fast march. Instead, it represents empowerment, which is the action of changing someone else's situation. African cosmology defines human actions by focusing on change and the affirmation that it can bring about more change. Blacks used the Hoodoo as a way to "handle" oppression the same way they used it to express that oppression with the blues.

Tips for understanding the Hoodoo

Perhaps you're wondering: Are you still confused? There is no hoodoo or voodoo. They are two different things. Although the latter originates in East Africa, magic found here comes directly from the African American culture. It has been influenced by magic books and native American cultures.

One of the most widespread hoodoo traditions is to use a mojo bag made with Flannel. The fabric in red is most commonly used to attract affection. It can also be used with talismans or herbs to bring money. However, when it is necessary to control another person, these elements may be mixed with items that are personal to the person. The bag is commonly used in rituals, and is worn by people who wish to achieve certain goals or tasks.

A subject of superstition and venerated for centuries, the black cats are an important part of hoodoo magic. They are used to attract famed or former lovers. However the extraction process can be quite terrifying. It is believed that boiling the cat to extract its bones and throwing them in a river was the traditional method to extract the bone. The only bone that floated was the one chosen for rituals. The situation is not good.

John the Conqueror is an African American folklore legend whose name was used to invent the name of a root commonly used in hoodoo. The ginger family plant is dried until it looks like two roasted testicles. The herb is used to alleviate stomach pains. This element can also be used in the mentioned mojo bag.

Hoodoo magic draws on a European influence, which can be found in grimoires (ancient wizard books), and also the Bible. Hoodoo is actually a form of magic which has a remarkable ability to use Biblical figures in its spells. Psalm 45-46 are used for reconciliation, 61 for protection of your home, and 121 for overnight security.

Bottle trees

East Africa, and especially the Congo, have promoted the custom of placing empty glasses bottles on branches of trees at night. This can be used to attract night demons. The glass traps them until the sun rises. Because cobaltblue bottles are the color that connects earth and sky, all colors can still be used.

THE VOODOO AND VODUN RELIGION

Voodoo & the Vodun religion

Voodoo practices are common in many parts of the world, especially on Haiti, Africa, New Orleans and Africa. Voodoo can conjure images of the dead. Voodoo may also invoke images of magic rituals, animals sacrificed, zombies, and dolls with pins. Voodoo practices vary depending on the locales they are used.

The Yoruba people (also known Aku or Lucumi), are the roots of Vodun (voodoo) religion. They can often be found in West Africa (Nigeria, Benin, Togo, Sierra Leone) at the Niger River.

Imported slaves mixed their religion with Catholic beliefs to form the Yoruba populace. This created a hybrid religion on Haiti, Vodun.

Vodun religion has its foundations in Yoruba religion. Vodun refers to "spirit", and although there are many who claim the Vodun religion belongs to "black magic" (magic used negatively to affect people), Vodun worship is part and parcel of "white magic". Only "bad" sorcerers, the Bokor, use rituals that are dark to their advantage.

A Vodun temple called Comfort has at its heart an altar decorated in candles and sacred objects. This is where God, and the spirits, communicate with men.

The vodun religion is home to many spirits, which are referred by the term Loa (mystery). They are invoked or nurtured during voodoo/voodoo rituals. It is believed that there are supernatural forces present in people, plants, and objects. Voodoo is celebrated on many occasions. It's used to celebrate births, death, and marriages as well as to invoke the Loa to assist and feed him. According to this religion every person would possess two spirits: a great protector spirit and a smaller guardian. The little guardian could leave the body during sleep or other rituals and be captured by the Loa.

Some Loa deities can be called Afra or Asojano, Afreqete (Helios), and Afreqete (Afreqete).

The voodoo priests, if men, are called human. If women are involved, they may be called mambo. Voodoo rites last for one whole night and are organized in the following:

The ritual includes sacred songs and drum rolls throughout. Of increasing size, the smallest one is called bula while the middle is called the second. And the largest, the madman, is the largest.

French dances known as Arara are accompanied with physical beatings.

Sacrificial animals such like chickens, goats and dogs are killed during the ritual. Blood from these animals is sometimes drunken and poured into ground to nourish Loa.

The use of extracts taken from herbs, spices, drug and other substances.

Each loa features a different type of drum sound and a certain sacrificial or animal.

A ritual may cause a dancer into a trance. They can feel convulsions or tremors and then be possessed by the Loa, the spirit that communicates with all the villages through their bodies. These people can be in a trance for up to 24 hours. However, it can last as long as several days.

The zombies

The dark side of vodun is the "black magic," which, as mentioned earlier, can create the dead or Zombies.

In reality, Bokor sorcerers and voodoo practitioners use a powder called "tetrodotoxin". This poison is extracted from pufferfish. It can cause a state that induces a state in which the body goes into a state of trance if taken in small doses.

Wade Davis discovered this way of creating zombies in 1924.

Voodoo dolls

A doll known as dagida in voodoo is very popular. It is used in hate rituals.

Inside the doll there is an object (or parts) of the victim.

The agenda represents the soul and will of the "victim". The sorcerer will continue to repeat magical phrases during rituals of love, or hate.

The ritual is over. The doll is wrapped with a red sheet if the doll has gone through a love ceremony or black if the doll has been subjected to a hated ritual.

CURIOSITY

The "National Voodoo Day," which was held in Haiti on January 10, 1996, attracted thousands of people who sang and danced their hearts out in celebration of Daagbo Hounon Houna. He was the supreme leader and sacrificed a goat to the Loa.

Numerous images showing the voodoo ceremony, the altar, initiation, and possessed by Loa can be found on the haitisurf site. External link.

Hoodoo or Voodoo

Hoodoo's beliefs came first to New Orleans from Haitian slaves during the early 1800s.

Hoodoo or huge is not a religion similar to voodoo. It is a set African-American rituals and is part black magic. It includes many rituals that combine botanical knowledge of Indian-American origin with American, Jewish folklore. Christian

Hoodoo may have been born in Africa. It was first recorded in 1981. Hoodooism became a synonym. Some claim that voodooism (or hoodoo) is actually a synonym for voodoo.

Voodoo or hoodoo may have a common roots, according to slaves

The most widely used symbol of the Hoodoo is the "bag", or mojo. It is a flannel sack with herbs and roots, as well as coins, and other "magic items" for creating potions.

Hoodoo has a goal to improve our daily lives with almost medical benefits. The supernatural forces acting on love, health and work are some examples. People have blood, nails hair, urine and blood. There are also objects such candles, incenses oil, oil, and powders used to make potions.

The roots

Voodoo, which blends African religion and spiritism, is well-known for its spiritual expression. However, shamanism is often mixed with witchcraft.

Voodoo practitioners believe they can choose between two worlds. Death is said to cause us to be separated from the invisible world, which corresponds a place where our departed mother and father keep an eye over everything.

The growth of voodoos

Voodoo continues to grow. Voodoo has been practiced most often in West Africa. Louisiana, Haiti, and West Africa are three of the most common locations. Only descendants are allowed to practice voodoo in West Africa. Cuba, Brazil and Dominican Republic also qualify.

The unique god

Many people who practice voodoo believe there is one higher being.

Loa (Iwa)

Many of the world's voodoo experts are well-known because they can communicate with lower level spirit beings.

The relationship to a loa

Voodoo practitioners believe a connection can also be made to a loa for advice and learning from its past. The connection with these entities is only spiritual.

Laos & Nature

According to one theory, all loans are linked to nature in some manner. Ogou for example is a male loa who rules iron because of his strength.

However, since 1987, Haitian constitutions have protected voodoo. This was not the case in all cases. The Catholic Church considered the voodoo-cult a hindrance to its faith, so the clergy set fires at the shrines and almost executed the priests.

Voodoopuppen

It is impossible to find voodoo dolls which correspond to real life. Although dolls exist, their association with African folk magic is known as "hoodoo" is stronger. These dolls are used to curse other people. They are often made of corn, potatoes, plants, or clothing.

Voodoo's basic features

The main points of voodoo ideology and the most important guiding principles for life:

Respect and veneration for Grand Met. To the Bondye, our supreme arbiter of destiny.

Respect, honor, faithful, and faithful service towards Lwa ("Lua= deity saint, god), protectors for the individual, group, and community

Respect for the Deceased

Respect, honor. Obeyance and assistance to the older, patriarchs and Matriarchs of your family and the local community.

Generosity and peaceful coexistence with both neighbors and foreigners is a hallmark of generosity.

Solidarity and faithful support at all levels, including friendship and kinship, is essential.

Voodoo Hierarchical Aspects

This religion has a very dictatorial nature. Gods can punish people with excessive punishments, fear and machismo. Although it is rooted in Africa, this religion attracts and fascinates through the beauty and music of the liturgical ceremonies. Let's not discuss the idea of a temple as a typical feature of this religion. Let us instead focus on autonomous brotherhoods each with its own style, traditions, and ways of doing things. Ahoumfort is one name for the voodoo altar. It is a religious place that can be compared to a playground once occupied the members of the extended familia (big family). The number, arrangement, and ornamentation in ranches that make up the voodoo Sanctuary depend on the financial resources available to the priest/priestess and to a lesser extent on their imaginations and the tastes they attribute to Gods.

You can recognize an ahoumfort only by looking at the peristyle. A covered area that is open to the elements, it's an open space in which dances and ceremonies are held. It is supported by several poles covered in different colors or motifs. The central one, the Poteaumitan is the pivot of ritual dancings. It symbolises the path of Gods from distant Guinea, to reach Haiti. The Perystile is the place for sick visitors or those who have come from far away or unemployed initiates, or just a place to rest when there are no ceremonies. The Perystile is usually found near the room de la mysterychambre des mysteres. Here are the altars for the Luas protectors. This room is filled with many objects, such as sacred stones or stamps, items of worship, brandy bottles and herbal medicine. Houngans or mambos Priests/priestesses are not an organized body. Rather, they are heads and members of brotherhoods than members of a hierarchical clergy. James et al. Comment: Everyone can houngan/mambo, provided they meet the essential requirements. These include being adept and knowing well the voodoo Liturgy, attributes to the gods, symbols, but most importantly going through the Kanzo initiation rites. Each shrine is organized according to hierarchy. One mambo or a houngan preside at each shrine.

Head of the choir at a voodoo group, the houguenikon. This can be a male or female. The la-place, an additional element of the hierarchy, is able to assume the title of master ceremonies if the hougenikon is in charge leases (gods), and interprets the appropriate ritual song. He greets all the spirits by opening the processions with his machete. The final rung of this ladder is the house. This can be of either sex, and is open to anyone who has completed the initiation. They make their living by treating the sick. Although they state that they are able to cure only supernatural diseases (insanity and epilepsy) the main source of income for the houngan as well as the mambo. You can also make a living by divination services, which are usually very costly. The fearsome personalities of the houngan or mambo can be seen in their personality traits. They are often very sensitive and can get angry easily. But, it is worth noting that the majority of houngans tend to homosexuality.

The mambo is mostly made up of women, and they have strong personalities. Bothhoungans as well as mambos. They are vindictive. The vocation can also include ambition, a craving for power, and avarice. These characters are only controlled by the protector god houmfort.

Ceremony

When the drums make a sound, it is time to start the ceremony. The ceremonies strengthen the ties with the horse.

All sacrifices are made and delivered in a variety offering. The majority of sacrifices are made with the animal's blood. Blood is the element that gives most power. During preparation for the rites it is common for the leader to invoke Thelua principle. He or she owns the head of the houngan. Thatluaprovides all necessary details to make sure the ceremonies go smoothly. This includes how the animals will be sacrificed and where they will be sacrificed. Thelua uses several techniques in every ceremony, but the most important is symbolic drawing.

Purification of animals to sacrifice takes place either one day beforehand or the same as the sacrifice. Without this condition, the offering cannot go to the deity. The animals remain tied to various posts around the enclosure. The houngan crouchs in front the main pole known as poto.

mitan, by which the leases can see operations that are done in their favor. The container containing purifying water is at the bottom of the post. A member of the orchestra chants an invocation, and the houngan then begins to sing a song. The orchestra plays to the beats, and the fastest announces that operations must be completed with greater speed. Blackbirds intended for sacrifice are brought first. After that, four-legged mammals are brought. The ceremony allows for baptism, blessing, healing, and veneration of the lua.

Ritual Sacrifices

Most ceremonies include an offering of an animal or animals for sacrifice to the leases. The animals should be the preferred or required color by God. The sacrifice needs to be prepared in advance. Invocations and prayers to the goddess must be made. Never slaughtered an animal.

The altar to worship leases

The stone representing the voodoo Gods must be submerged in water or an alcohol drink. The liquid contained in the container must be replaced from time. The basic elements of its upper portion are red, green, and black flags. Hanging chains can also be found in descending orders. You should place fresh foods, such as goat meat, yams or edible tuber, and various kinds of sweet flour, at its feet. There should always be printed images of the saints.

The leases for the voodoo faith are divided into 2 large groups: Lua-rada and Lua-petro. The first is the gods that come from Guinea. These gods are kind gods. They can also punish their believers with death but they are trustworthy and just gods. Instead, the gods Petro immediately conjure up images of unflinching strength, toughness and determination. They are gods that devotees compare to the rigid rada gods. Without exception, the malefic geniuses in leases Petro that bear the adjective of red eyes, (hehruj), are those with the heh-ruj. Alua petro They have the same name, followed by a nickname, (Danballah flangbo Ogou yansan Ezili -mapyang). There are leases to whites as well as blacks and mulattos. Some are twins as in the Marassa. There are leases for men and leases for women. The leases are there.

One of most prominent families is that Ogun. It is a legionnaire divinity who is honored as the blacksmith for the world. The ethnic origin has seen significant changes. This was because the Voodooists attach greater significance to the character a lua and his particular tastes rather than to specific functions that tradition attributes; that is why we can search.

Ogun, also known as Ogun del monte, is wearing a red shirt that has black motifs and cortege pants. A machete is one of his distinguishing features.

Ogun batala, Ercili's hubby, dresses up in white just like Ercili. He doesn't drink alcohol, something that was rejected by the saint. He represents the brand with a handshake and a cap that is high.

According to Santiago Apostol and San Jacobo el Mayor's popular chromolithography, an Ogun legionnaire is shown wearing a red cap on its head and holding a logo in his hand.

Ogun Del Rio, a submarine saint, is his name. Its distinctive feature is freshwater.

Ogun Chal's kleptomaniac rates are what sets him apart from the other Oguns. He steals to share with his sisters what he has taken.

Senche. It is believed there is an affiliation relationship between Cemiche & Senche. In which the father of the alternate is the first, however, this is symbolic. Senche gets to guarantor the dead while the first gets them in the cemetery. This proves that the person is really a failure and has thrown the ground on him. Lacua finally appears and crosses him.

Gran Bua, who is the family's owner, can be punctuated by other leases. This is because they are Gran Bua, Gran Bua, and have to ask for similar authorization to conduct any activity in the mountain. Togo, also known as the Butcher, is well-known for his partiality. Yudon is responsible for guiding the other saints.

A few submarine saints can also be worshiped similarly.

Zau Pemba, endowed to prominent powers in order of an intelligence ordering, is the basis on which Zau organizes and directs all healings.

Simbi is known to be the guardian over the sources and the swell.

Ercili (also Erzuli known) is the goddess fertility, love, passion, and she's also lust.

Two marine deities are so similar that they're often worshiped together, and even celebrated with the exact same song: the Mermaid or the Whale of The Ocean. Some believe the Whale to be the Mermaid's mother, while others say she is her hubby. However, there are many other names that can be used to describe the same divinity.

The Mermaid depicted in this image is a beautiful woman without branches and a mortal torso. However, she is only held by a young kittenish woman when she enters the sanctuary. She is famous for her ability in the ocean to bring her wealth and fortune. She is the owner of the ocean's treasures. Her underwater mansion brims with gold and valuable artifacts that were salvaged from sinking ships.

Agwe, the swell's sovereign. He represents the ocean's intuitive power and in-depth understanding. Age, the husband and father of the Mermaid.

Filomez, who is a water spirit is given flowers when she gets possession. He may also use a broom or sweep out all negativity and bad fortune. It is her passion to share dreams with people is what she is most known for.

Another family we find the Guede amongst their distinguished ranks

Lacrua refers to the spirit that was the first person to enter a cemetery.

Zombie has been anthropomorphized as an old man, with a wrinkled visage, who transforms when he is in, or possesses someone. He is an avid mountain dweller. Some consider him a maroon martyr who would prefer to live in the backwoods, regardless of how remote. He weaves clothes by picking grapevines. He's not a living man and he stayed on the mountain.

Cimitier (the name of this lua) seems to derive its name form cemetiere (cemetery), the cemetery where the saint's hearthstone is located.

Saints of the roads.

Legba guardian over the doors and substantial portion of the Hounfor. It is the first to invoke it and the last one to be dismissed. The priest of the gods. It is the one responsible for opening the fence that separates world of mortals from world of the transcendent. Also, this bone allows contact with other spirits.

Lua Chemin. Donate to charity

Lua Calfu means the one with the four roads. His food can go anywhere, but his balcony needs to be against a wall.

Slow, it is aware that he was not able to work for long periods of time. It lives in an area near the entry door to the dwelling and provides some protection to the occupants.

Cole- Cord, which is the name we offer, corresponds to a Tropological pronunciation of ours. This information was used to create the name. They have confirmed that the closest meaning is that of knot, or landing, at the entrance to a house.

Other leases

Ayizan is a spirit that guides initiates to wisdom. Guidance the first steps towards Truth. Leghba's woman. It's Erzulie's hand that is believed to have the ability scarify evil spirits.

Alegda refers to a lua evil and stressed, which is a source for wrong and life.

Zaca means the lua of land husbandry, growth, substance.

Bossu is a turtle-related creature. According to this reason, the turtle can be considered a sacred creature.

Dan home or Dan lady water are benevolent divinities and wealth dispensers. It's the sacred Boa, and loves sticky places.

Loko is the owner/operator of the trees. He has a profound influence on healers who use sauces.

Lenglesu can be described as a Linguistic Devil. It is both violent and devilish. Any commitment that's broken to him can lead to his death. Lenglesu can be presented as thelua, the rainbow, and Blinginsu Mars or walks with him. There are two Lenglesu Lenglesu Damasas.

Djab Monane, it is a luadevil he called at midnight, the center of the mountain

Saint Michel Archangel, lua to be kept at your door. Bad currents can be stopped or defeated.

Macuto, or Macuto the Machete-wielding Man is a man who carries a machete and a Yaba.

Zombies

A zombie, also known as "zombie" or "zombie", is a legendary figure that originates in areas where Voodoo worship is common. It's about a sorcerer that uses magic to revive a dead man and enslave him. Popular belief is that a bokor, or vaudoo sorcerer can resurrect dead people who are subject to the will and power of the one who brings them back to life through a ritual. It can even transform him into werewolf.

Hoodoo is a form folk magic that was created in the south-eastern United States. The Hoodoo combines elements from several cultures such as African, European (especially Cajun and Roma traditions), Native American. It is not associated with any religious traditions, and it is not a faith. It is a syncretic form of magic, developed over time in America from the interaction with multiple cultures. It is sometimes considered one of the "sources" for hoodoo magical magic. In fact, there are multiple independent magical strands. These strands have however joined the voodoo and hoodoo covenants to protect their fellows and frequently exchange spells. Although it is rare to find wizards who are proficient in only one of the strands of magic without more detailed knowledge, it is more common to find magicians who have syncretic knowledge. They draw inspiration from many folk magic forms while staying true to their beliefs (e.g. A magician might be able to recognize Wiccan magic as well as Hoodoo. However, the source of his powers, or his ancestors, are marked. The rituals mark that the source of the magician's power is then replaced with the one which he believes. These are just a few examples of these strands.

Magic created by the Santa Muerte Clio

Wiccan

Native American Shamanism

In the United States, as elsewhere in the world, a unique body of magic knowledge was developed. These magical skills could be taught in similar ways in schools and universities. However small, nomadic communities were able to pass on their knowledge by word of mouth. This has led to travelers from all cultures and places to be able to mix parts of their native knowledge with information that was not there in the beginning. Hoodoo doctors in the past were frequently mobile, offering services in various cities. Later and rarely, they stopped permanent in specific places to operate shops for the sale of the huge range of products involved in this magic system. These hoodoo traces are found in Alabama (Georgia), Arkansas, Florida, Mississippi and South Carolina. They can also be found in Tennessee,

Tennessee, Tennessee, Tennessee, Tennessee, and Illinois. Many kinds of magic are given the label of Hoodoo, but what they share is the concept that trust in God's providence is essential for justice. This idea is far more important than any of the small and large religions from the Hoodoo's origin. It is the highest common factor in all religions. However, it is less common among atheist groups that have a particular religious knowledge, such as the Christian.

This characteristic makes it possible for hoodoo to combine many different beliefs. the uniting of different religious elements into a common belief. Hoodoo, which is unlike other types of magic can be learned by anyone, although it has the inherent limitation of being taught to people who believe in concepts like luck and bad fortune, an independent justice higher than man. Hoodoo can be used to gain access to any supernatural forces that may exist to improve your life in all areas, including money, love (or lack thereof), work, health, and money.

Hoodoo magicians have been confined to the US south but their wanderlust made it possible for them to survive in cities with high cultural diversity. New York is a perfect example. Because it is the place where many traditions meet, it has been able to become the center for any small Hoodoo Coven that currently resides at the Bronx.

Creole voodoo in New Orleans often includes the Louisiana spell. This is known as Hoodoo. Hoodoo has elements of Voodoo. Hoodoo can be considered a complement to Voodoo. Voodoo as well as Hoodoo can be distinguished. Hoodoo's uniqueness is that it doesn't differentiate between black magic and white magical. It includes all forms and types of magic. Hoodoo and Voodoo are often combined. Hoodoo is a complicated magic method

Hoodoo Symbols

Voodoo might be described as religion, and Hoodoo as magic system. Voodoo refers to "the spirit God". Voodoo strongly believes in the existence and power of a God. These powerful spirits care about everyday matters such as love, money, and family. However, the rituals and spells that invoke the loa do not have to be used regularly.

Hoodoo is the magic from southern America. Hoodoo is designed to help you harness the power of supernatural forces to improve your life. Hoodoo can also help to attract luck, wealth and fortune-telling in order to increase your power.

Hoodoo's ingredients

It's possible, like many magic practices to make extensive use herbs, minerals animal parts, personal propriety, as well bodily fluids such as menstrual blood, urine and semen.

Hoodoo tradition's important practices for communication with ancestors, spirits and the dead are well-known. Hoodoo magic includes the recitation of Psalms.

It can also be used to describe the magic system ("hoodoo") as well as the practitioner ("it is the hoodoo guy !").." It can be used both as a noun ("he Hoodooed that") and an adjective ("it's all hoodoo!"). ").

Hoodoo has always been a central theme in blues. Ma Rainey's Louisiana Hoodoo Blues, Arthur Crudups Hoodoo Lady Blues, and many other examples are just some of the examples. In blues songs, other than the usual hoodoo or mojo terms there are many words such as jinxes, goofer dust and so on.

Hoodoo New Orleans draws heavily from European folklore, African folklore, Kabbalistic influences as well Native American herbalism. It includes elements of Christianity as well Jewish mysticism and symbols. The Bible is seen as both a magical talisman or a source of magic powers. Hoodoo practice relies on the Psalms and Saints. Talismans may contain the body parts or organs of monstrous animals such as bayous alligator claws, chicken feet, and chicken feet.

Bewitchments stem from African folk practices, such as crossing and uncrossing or using spiritual baths. Hoodoo is a New Orleans tradition that requires knowledge.

Voodoo welcomes everyone in New Orleans. Voodoo does NOT require a formal religious ritual of initiation, nor any strict orthodoxy. There are no rules for practicing this worship. Voodoo can be used by all people regardless if they are of the same race, creed, religion, or origin. It is flexible, adaptable, and syncretic. All terms that describe the spiritual powers of the archetypal divine Voodoo, are interchangeable. Voodoo practice can be done in infinite ways, depending on each individual's culture and geographical origins.

New Orleans was an important port that allowed many cultures to come together. The many influences that had a profound impact on New Orleans Voodoo have been so varied. One example of this is the Cuban-inspiring Santeria and the initiations for the Mambos. Another example are the Obeah women of the Antilles (namely Belize or the Bahamas), as well the followers and supporters of various Churches spirits. Finally, there's the Hoodoo that includes superstitions and spells. New Orleans Voodoo incorporates spirituality as well as herbalism. Saint Voodoos include, for instance, the famed

Indian Chief Black Hawk. He also takes part in ritual work. New Orleans Voodoo is a Louisiana French Creole language.

A brief history and description of slavery

Voodoo was brought from West Africa to French Louisiana by slaves, workers, and other servants. The majority of African slaves expelled to Louisiana in the period 1719-1731 came from Benin, where they were deported mainly by Fon people. All contributed to their cultural practices. All three ethnicities contributed to Louisiana Voodoo. They are vital to Louisiana voodoo's knowledge regarding poisons as well as herbalism. Louisiana Voodoo first became popularized in 1800. Slave community quickly outnumbered white settlers. This is how the slave community was dominated over the new arrivals. A 1731-1732 census revealed that the ratio between African slaves, European settlers, was over two to 1. Due to the small number settlers being slave owners or planters, Africans were kept within large groups. This allowed them keep African culture. Southern Louisiana has preserved the culture & languages of slave families more than other states. French code and Catholic influence ban the sale to their families of child slaves.

Catholicism & Syncretism

Many Africans were forced into conversion to Catholicism by the owners of their slaves, who forbade them from practicing Vodou. This has led the Voodoo spirits to be merged with Christian saints' names and traits. Voodoo survived the persecution of Catholicism and continued to exist as a religion.

High mortality rates in slavery gave slave survivors an instinct for initiation, and solidarity. "Cohesive functional society" was born from the lack of fragmentation among the slave community as well as the kinship system created through the hardships of slavery. It is well-integrated.

Voodoo of the early Louisiana was known for its custom of wearing and creating talismans, or amulets, to heal, protect, or cause damage to others. The Ouanga had poisonous root from the CursedFig tree. It was used as a charm to poison enemies. It is a tree which was brought from Africa and kept at Louisiana. The protection of God was often mentioned by ritual administrators, as well as Jesus.

New Orleans Voodoo offers a unique experience that is not found in other forms. New Orleans Voodoo is now influenced by 19th-century spiritualism. The use of "spirit guides" during worship and ritual possession is a unique feature of this "spiritual", African American "spiritual" religion. Voodoo was a spiritual practice which has had an impact on the New Orleans Spiritual Churches.

Louisiana Voodoo also includes ancestral worship which is also from West Africa. It emphasizes the importance of respecting elders. Older enslaved Louisiana Creole residents had a higher survival rates.

Legend says that Marie Laveau reigned as New Orleans' voodoo princess during the height of voodoo use. You can also make voodoo-dolls out of gray grays. It's a type of magic talismanic. The term gris-gris refers to gray. It's a mix of black or white. Gris Gris could be used both as a noun nor a verb.

Voodoo figurines were traditionally used to worship or house deities. Voodoo practitioners often view them as an object of vengeance. However, many work together to protect them from any malicious use. Ninety per cent of New Orleans' voodoo practices are focused on healing and finding true love. New Orleans voodoo figurines are often made into fashion accessories and souvenirs.

Voodoo zombies

New Orleans Voodoo believes in zombies. A zombie describes a person that has been resurrected after having been buried. After resurrection, the person who became a zombie is still controlled and directed by others. It does not possess any will.

A zombie can be described as a living individual who has never been harmed. Instead, she is a zombie who has been given powerful drugs by an evil wizard. Many believe in zombies but have never seen one.

The Queens of Voodoo

In 1808, the United States approved the Embargo Bill. The Queens in Voodoo, who were well-known because of their immense power, played an important part at many ceremonies, rituals and dances. They attracted crowds numbering in the hundreds of thousands. They were practitioners who sold and administered amulets and "grisgris", charms, magic powders, and other magical items. They were able, among other things, to heal and fulfill their needs.

These women were Creole and African, and they were strong leaders in a society where slavery was a system that oppressed blacks and whites. Their influence is also related to the city's historical past. The French colonial area had a large and diverse population of people of color, which was granted specific rights. They were eligible to purchase property and pursue higher education in New Orleans. It was possible for women of color to have significant influence over spiritual leaders. This advantage was also available for free women. Women of extraordinary power must be able to keep the religious traditions of West Africa as well as Central Africa preserved.

Marie Laveau (one of 15 "voodoo Princesses") that were found around 19th Century New Orleans was the most powerful, prominent, and well-known among them all. Marie Laveau's religious ritual at Lake Pontchartrain on the morning of Saint John's Day (1874) attracted 12,000 both black and non-white people. Legend has it that she was visited at least once by businessmen, politicians and lawyers before any financial or business decisions were made. Although she was impartial and non-discriminatory in her assistance, she may prefer slaves to "wealthy or influential clients". Marie Laveau's 'powerful charms' Marie Laveau was once the most powerful voodoo leader of New Orleans. His influence led to the adoption of Catholic practices in Voodoo beliefs systems. Marie Laveau's compassion and kindness for the less fortunate is well-known.

Marie Laveau, a hairdresser, also had an impact on her clients. She was up to date on all gossip in the city. She was also a trusted source of potions or voodoo dolls for her customers. His legacy can be seen today. His grave is the oldest in the cemetery and is a popular tourist attraction. The cemetery is visited by Voodoo believers who offer gifts and pray to the spirit of their leader. These offerings will expedite Queen Voodoo. Saint Expedite means the spirit that is between death, and life. The chapel which now houses the statue was once used by funerals. Marie Laveau remains an important figure in Louisiana voodoo, and New Orleans culture. Multiple reports have suggested Marie Laveau is the Voodoo king, as players shout her name while rolling their dice.

Hoodoo & the voodoo magic

Louisiana residents often use voodoo magic for their unique New Orleans Creole Voodoo. Hoodoo practitioners sometimes include elements of Voodoo. Others do not. Hoodoo does NOT resemble Voodoo. Voodoo has nothing to do with Hoodoo. Both are complementary, however they are completely different. Hoodoo, unlike Voodoo, includes both white magic and dark magic. Voodoo relates to religion, while Hoodoo relates to magic.

How to make Voodoo dolls

Purification is the initial step.

Purification involves the removal of energy from the material. It is also known by neutralization. Many dolls made from these items can be manufactured by industry. These include threads, buttons and glue as well as fabric and buttons.

There are many ways you can cleanse your body: salt, sandalwood oils and frankincense. Salt, sandalwood oils, frankincense or earth

The second step is making a doll.

This refers both to the author's thought process and state of energy. Shop dolls may not be as strong as dolls made with your own hands if you follow all rules. The image you have in your mind when creating a doll should be the most important. This must be clearly defined in your mind. It shouldn't be mixed up with your emotions.

You want financial success, luck and prosperity. Your doll should constantly think about money, loan repayments, financial situations, and other financial issues. to improve your financial condition. Making dolls involves every word, tone. Power, voice, volume, and any action. It's not okay to be silent. However, it is important to not curse and shout at others who cause your problems.

This is the final stage.

To light the candle, you will need to place it on top of your doll. Add pine needles, dried sage, and pine needles to your fire. Place the doll directly over the fire.

This should be repeated seven additional times. After the ceremony, the doll is yours. It should not be revealed to anyone.

The process of making a Voodoo doll

The New Orleans branch is home to the classic Voodoo doll. The following items are required:

2 sticks

Rope or lanyard

Cloth

Glue

2 buttons

Clothing for one person, or hair and nails, etc.

It is very easy to create voodoo puppets with any of the materials available. It can sometimes be difficult to find Spanish moss, which is so popular in New Orleans. The moss is easily replaced with straw and cotton. Let's now see step-by, how to draw a vaudoo doll.

A cross is made initially from two sticks. After that, it's glued with a string. The wax helps strengthen the fastening. Before you apply the wax to your cord or lace, you'll need to rub it with some wax. The cross can then easily be wrapped in moss. Make sure that you use only large, strong pieces to prevent moss from being broken. To wrap the doll's neck, cut the fabric into long straight strips. Now, you can create the doll's face. Eyes can be made of buttons or beads. The threads are used in embroidery the mouth. Next, give your doll the energy and personality that you would like. Attach a tuft hair from a certain person to the doll's skull. The doll's skull is covered with blood. Pieces of clothing from the person are then added.

Wood's dolls represent one of the most dangerous symbols in African religions. They also have a large influence on Western culture. The general public considers drugs, sorcery, demagoguery and deminism one thing.

What exactly does a Voodoo doodoo toy look like?

They can be used in many ways today, regardless of how ancient they were. They are made by New Orleans, America's center for voodoo. The first was gris-gris. Grisgris refers to a word that can be translated as "gray", which suggests they are somewhere in between black and white witchcraft. Grigris could be either a noun nor a verb. It refers both to ritual objects such as dolls or cloth bags that are filled with magic ingredients. New Orleans has four major types of grisgris: Love money finance domination and curse raising. These are some of the most sought-after voodoo or grisgris dolls.

Voodoo dates back approximately 7000 years. Voodoo, which means spirit or mystery, is a term used to describe the practice. Voodoo practitioners believe in God, and that under him are powerful spirits known by loa (loa). Voodoo perfume has all you need to live a happy and fulfilled life. Loa is slightly unlike the Catholic saints of angels and Christian Christians in that they ask for your help but don't request it.

Vodun religion was brought to slaves by African slaves. It was mixed in with European folkmagic and superstition. The African Borrowing Religion resulted from this religious mix. In 1782 Louisiana's governor ban the import from West Indies any black slaves. Louisiana's governor considered Voodoo hazardous to civilians. In an effort to stop slave rebellion, a governor demanded that Voodoo is banned. Voodoo now represents a major method of resistance of slaves against oppression by their owners. This resistance was strengthened through the support from God of War which enabled them to be freed.

Voodoo came out as a very violent religion, and was persecuted throughout the colonial period. Christians were forced kill priests, their followers, and to destroy their temples due to their threat. Slave owners were made to baptize any children they brought with them upon arrival in Haiti and America in the Roman Catholic Church tradition. Voodoo worshippers went underground, worshipping in secret their ancestral spirits and gods. Ironically Catholicism provided a cover for Voodoo as the saints of Africa merged into Catholicism. The new Voodoo preserved the original African slave deities and synthesized these in the new voodoo.

Voodoo remains a vital part of many people's spiritual lives in West Africa, Haiti, and in certain States of the United States even after more than 400 years.

There are many types of Voodoo dolls.

Doll: A family heirloom passed down generation after generation. The Louisiana Broomstick doll. Louisiana's broom symbolizes health and abundance. They can also help eliminate negative effects from the home. These dolls were inspired from South African folklore. Broom dolls, small brooms used to protect, heal and increase abundance are known as broom dolls. They are very close to European straw-dolls.

Ju Ju doll. Ju Ju dolls provide protection and good luck. JuJu, a doll consecrated to protect against bad luck and other unfortunate events, is called a Ju Ju doll. These dolls may be used to protect your home against evil.

Today, the most sought after voodoo doll goals are love and fortune, wealth, power, dominance power, protection, removal, and healing. They are still used to exact justice. They do not forget their responsibility. GriGri could be described as a charm and amulet that brings luck or love to the owner. They can be used in creative visualization to help you focus on any goal.

New Orleans' Voodoo dolls are a popular wedding gift. They are often given to guests at the ceremony. Old TraditionVoodoo Hood stipulates that each guest must wish the couple happiness before they're given out. It is believed that a doll can ruin a marriage. A pin can be attached at any doll's part. However, it can also be attached in some locations to increase the desire. To make sure that the doll is able to have many children, you can attach a pin to the pocket of a bride's doll. After all guests have expressed their happiness, it is time for the ceremony to be over. The bride's doll is presented to the groom's. These dolls will be taken into their new homes to ensure a happy and prosperous future. This ceremony is for the couple who wants it.

The Voodoo doll. These dolls help to support a specific area of the wearer's life. Many artists are inspired to make voodoo toys based upon the ideas of the gods, gods, and spirits. Doll Jester. Jester doll is an older form of the voodoo doll. It looks like a male in clothes. These dolls are symbolic of harmony between emotions and thoughts in meditation. They can be either black and white. To prevent any damage or curses, it is possible to make the right side black. You can make the right side red or white to help spirits and love spells. This doll's back has a blue color and is used to attract luck.

Other voodoo-dolls have more specific features and are often bought by collectors who know the risks associated to owning them. Whatever the purpose of your doll, you must treat it with respect. All of them are objects of ancient magic. Creativity.

Voodoo toys can be made out of any kind of material. These dolls are made from thread or sewn, and some have embroideries on their faces. The doll's appearance speaks volumes to its intended purpose. A doll who is full of abundance might have large breasts. Be careful! Your intentions and energy will be taken by the doll creating a positive atmosphere. Don't make dolls who have a problem. If you want to make the desired change, create a doll with the problem.

Important are the colors used in the doll's design. Yellow denotes success, understanding, charm, trust and trust. White represents peace.

Voodoo cleanse baths are another option.

Who is that Voodoo doll representing?

Ritual dolls used in witchcraft could also function as prototypes. They are a living representation of a particular person and act as a connection between the sorcerer of witchcraft and the victim. It can affect and impact the victim's mind.

An expert magician can easily make another person submit to his will. Does not work. A spell is one the most powerful types or sorcery. There are many rituals associated with volt exposure.

Let's now look at the many most well-known ones.

Rite for passage

Useful for husheing gossip or paralyzing a person's eloquence during a crucial moment. A touch of meat or clay is put into the doll's mouth.

Love spell using a Voodoo Doll

This ritual is one that black magicians consider to be the most powerful. To do this, you would need to light a red flame in the dark, speak a few lines, and drop some of your blood in the ritual doll's heart.

This is done by creating a volute that has sexually explicit characteristics. Once it's finished, the black thread is applied to the place. It is believed that this ritual will calm the person and prevent him from feeling the attraction towards the woman he has cheated.

Rituals of healing

Contrary to popular belief, magic spells can still be used for long-term purposes. It is possible to create a Volt by connecting bones from animal animals. The ritual doll should be a mirror image of the patient's names during the christening.

The doll should then go into the appropriate box to represent the coffin. It is believed that the doll and the disease will cause the patient to get cured.

Hoodoo Magic Protective Techniques

All rituals involving magic flow are linked to the most powerful and oldest flow. If you do not have enough experience, it is possible to accidentally awaken sinister forces that could later turn against you. It is best to be aware of the basic rules to prevent this.

1. Volt is not a weapon that can spread deadly disease to your opponent. Such rituals may result in severe illness or retribution.

2. There are no rituals that can be performed in the cemetery.

3. The vault cannot made with the cremation earth, because this might lead to the death the person who identified him.

Ingram Content Group UK Ltd.
Milton Keynes UK
UKHW022150170723
425288UK00015B/273